Fetish Style

Frenchy Lunning

BLOOMSBURY
LONDON · NEW DELHI · NEW YORK · SYDNEY

Bloomsbury Academic

An imprint of Bloomsbury Publishing Plc

50 Bedford Square	175 Fifth Avenue
London	New York
WC1B 3DP	NY 10010
UK	USA

www.bloomsbury.com

First published 2013

British Library Cataloguing-in-Publication Data
A catalogue record for this book is available from the British Library.

ISBN: HB: 978 1 84788 571 5
         PB: 978 1 84788 570 8
         epub: 978 0 85785 809 2

Library of Congress Cataloging-in-Publication Data
A catalog record for this book is available from the Library of Congress.

Typeset by Apex CoVantage, LLC, Madison, WI, USA
Printed and bound in Great Britain

Fetish Style

STANDARD LOAN

Books are to be returned on or before the last date below

Subcultural Style Series

ISSN: 1955-0629

Series editor: Steve Redhead, University of Ontario Institute of Technology

The *Subcultural Style* series comprises short, accessible books that each focus on a specific subcultural group and their fashion. Each book in the series seeks to define a specific subculture and its quest to exist on the fringes of mainstream culture, which is most visibly expressed within a subculture's chosen fashions and styles. The books are written primarily for students of fashion and dress but will also be of interest to those studying cultural studies, sociology, and popular culture. Each title will draw upon a range of international examples and will be well-illustrated. Titles in the series include: *Punk Style*, *Queer Style*, *Body Style*, and *Fetish Style*.

For Mistress Jean, Ron, Baby Dani, Rachel, Rio, Ursula and all my friends at Ground Zero. And of course, for my family, who support me in all things.

Contents

List of Illustrations

–1–

Introduction

Fetishism . . . offers parallels between late nineteenth and late twentieth century commodity cultures . . . The objectified female anatomy is sexually domesticated through
sartorial masquerades, just as the household fetishes of cars, TVs, and swimming pools
are shown to be sites of displaced lack, dream surrogates for better values.

William Pietz, *Fetishism as Cultural Discourse*[1]

Eyes widen and a slow tentative smile creeps up on the face of a person suddenly
very interested in what you have to say at the very mention of the word *fetish*. It has
stood for the most subversive, transgressive, and underground practice in Western
culture for more than a century. Although it is common to say that fetish practice is
misunderstood, the remarkable inclusion of fetish fashions in fashion runway shows
and the fetish-influenced performances created by rock musicians begin to reveal
the dubiousness, the embarrassing confusion, and the probable falsity of this claim.
Anyone who participates in even the most everyday commercial life in Western culture knows quite well what fetish is. Christians who venerate the cross as a symbol
of Christ's sacrifice, Packer football fans who wear yellow and green items, people
addicted to particular television shows, women who visit DSW regularly, and even
children who obsess over the latest video game all fetishize something—an object or a
performance or a narrative—that stands in for the complex constellation of meanings,
associations, and desires that the fetish pulls down from the imaginary into a phantasmic fulfilling though temporary reality. Yet the word is draped in dark associations. It
brings forth uncanny and threatening images of ball gags, transvestites, Leathermen,
imperious dominatrices, and the inference of extreme perversity—all of which are
indeed part of the fetish performance oeuvre.

How can we negotiate this distance, this yawning gap between the fetish as the
everyday fan practice and the haunting noir world of the S/M (sadomasochism) performance? Amanda Fernbach gives us a clue: Leopold von Sacher-Masoch's "novel
[*Venus in Furs*] closely echoes his real-life experiences as tyrannized slave to a powerful
woman . . . expressed through his penchant for theatricality, and he often dressed up as
a bear, bandit or servant."[2] In fact, it is through theatrical performance and, most particularly, through costume dressing—through fashion—that we can traverse easily from
one end of this spectrum to the other. Fashion in its performance as costume—whether
worn by models on the runway or drag queens and S/M slaves in the fetish clubs—is

the clothing of an actor playing a role: from the mainstream experience of fashion magazines, couture runway images online, or the lucky find in a consignment shop, extending to the darkest extreme of fashions emerging from the dungeons and clubs of the fetish underworld. Fashion itself, even in its most ubiquitous usage, *is in fact fetish*.

This work seeks to unravel and delineate those lines of connection and association between fashion and fetish that have been laid down through desire in the Western capitalist commodified cultures and histories in which they grew up, tangled in the desires, repressions, and obsessions of the subjects who formed as a consequence. In so doing, we will hold up the mirror to our own complicity and desires and force ourselves to acknowledge that fetish—as Marx rightly understood—was and is the condition of modern industrialized cultures, as is fashion.

The study of fetishism, in virtually every history written in contemporary times, begins with the progressive derivation of the word *fetish*. Clearly, this is a compelling way to track the complicated discursive adventure of taboo, transformation, and transnational exchanges that form the contemporary understanding of that term. The word forms an object, in a way, that allows us a narrative thread to pull forward from the nineteenth century, into our own time, and furthermore to begin to unravel its uniquely complex, interwoven, and largely misunderstood history with fashion. It begins and ends with the magical objects of the Other, and that is also what gives it its taboo status, its sexual sheen, and its remarkably sturdy formation in human culture throughout its relatively short history.

If one begins—as I did, sitting in an airport waiting for a flight—by circling the dates of the myriad sources in the bibliographies of the reference books on fetish, a very distinctive pattern becomes clear: the vast amount written about fetish occurs around two periods, separated almost exactly by 100 years: in the 1870s to around 1900 and in the 1970s through the first decade of the twenty-first century. Though there is a continual discussion that extends throughout the period, the bulk of it is clustered in the extreme end points of the late nineteenth and twentieth centuries. Each of these sites have clusters of iteration developed around very different points of discovery, however: in the emerging modernism of the late nineteenth century, the discourse of fetish is written by medical and newly forming psychiatric authorities, as well as through the new formations of advertising and magazines featuring fetish fashions, especially the corsets and high heels of women's clothing and the high collars of men. In the late twentieth century, just within the rupture that occurred between the modernist and postmodernist epistemes, fetish is once again obsessively written about, but this time by cultural studies scholars and, once again, the psychiatric critics and philosophers. As William Pietz states in the epigraph quote, these intersections are found in times of dense commodity formations in each culture. But each formation congeals its concepts, fears, and anguish paradoxically in the clothing of female fashion, using what has now become the taxonomy of fetish fashions: corsets, boots, masks, skinsuits, and technologies.

In this investigation, we will trace the meanings and forms of fetish from its origins in the colonial responses to African racial and religious practices to the outcomes in contemporary fashion cultures of this complexity of forms, performances, and iterations. And in so doing, we will "unlace" the tabooed term and allow it to breathe in a more informed, larger understanding of this complex concept.

Colonialism and the African Other

We begin by regarding fifteenth-century Africa, a largely unknown and certainly misunderstood location (then as now), where the *Encyclopedia Britannica* of 1800 located and defined the original term *fetichism* as

> a stage of worship, or of the ways of regarding nature (for in simple states of mind religion and philosophy are in great part merged) in which ordinary material objects are regarded as holding, or as being the vehicle of, supernatural powers and influences,—which powers and influences can, it is supposed, be controlled or directed by the person possessing the object so endowed.[3]

In other words, fetish at this time was considered by authorities to be a primarily religious object denigrated as trinket or "juju," endowed with magical and spiritual powers, that could summon up a sort of transforming "power" by an individual who held—or wore—the object. Further, this entry notes that by studying these "savages and uneducated peoples," they—the Western intellectuals and academic authorities (with a distinct sniff of superiority)—are doing the work of the social sciences in classifying these practices and through "resemblances to each other . . . to give a general name marking that resemblance. Such a name we have in 'fetichism.'" Additionally, this conclusion was identified through fetish's resemblance to "the talismans and charms common in Europe, and popular with sailors and travellers *[sic]* another group of uneducated and arguably 'savage' Others *above all men* [italics mine]."[4] Their correspondence to the Christian cross is not mentioned.

The encyclopedia continues to trace the word to its first acknowledged use in a "general sense" by Charles De Brosses. De Brosses, in his eighteenth-century work *Du Culte Des Dieux Fétiches* (1760), locates the fetish object as an essentially material, terrestrial entity[5] and firmly begins its designation as an object not innately embodied with spiritual or magical aspects or positioned as an idol. Furthermore, the *Encyclopedia Britannica* (1800) also establishes the link that will define the fetish as a taboo aesthetic associated with women but practiced by men:

> But the belief in the efficacy of peculiar objects upon a person's welfare is not by any means confined to savages. Witchcraft is a form of fetishism, and it can hardly be said to be dead from among us even now. Others than children may be found who will keep a crooked sixpence, a curious stone . . . for luck,—prompted by exactly those instincts, which although long superseded in some races, are perhaps the highest the savage possesses.[6]

The link to sailors and travelers who are "above all men" begins to create the myth of fetishism that Freud will establish as a distinctly transgressive and male condition. But the encyclopedia also notes the irresistible quality of the fetish object for all Europeans who were fascinated by the influx of objects from colonized and commodified Africa and Asia, which, as a result of the newly opened markets in these places, brought an irresistible explosion of exoticism into that culture of objects, radically changing the European and especially the French culture of the late nineteenth century.

The best example of this, of course, is cubism, created by Pablo Picasso with his landmark work *Les Demoiselles d'Avignon* (1907), which was—as the urban legend goes—supposedly influenced by his encounter with African masks. The fetishistic work further delineates feminine subjects as the fetish objects through Picasso's execution of the "Demoiselles" as nude prostitutes whose bodies are distorted by the analytic cubist tactic of multiplied perspectives: this positions the observer to view the entirety of the prostitutes' bodies in one all-consuming misogynistic viewpoint. Cubism was to become the key art historical aesthetic in twentieth-century modernism and particularly in its appropriation by advertising and illustration styles.

As William Pietz establishes, the African fetish, imported into Europe since the fifteenth century, refused to stay in place as "a safely displaced synecdoche of the Enlightenment's Other." It had the effect of "rubbing some of their exoticist aura off onto the Western objets d'art through the attraction of a 'defamiliarizing African idyll . . . [while] Africa was seen as prelinquistic, prerational, unskeptical, its "signs" naïve in their simplicity and mediated by sensualism.'"[7] The exoticism of African masks and Japanese ukiyo-e prints had a profound effect on European art. In the stale aesthetics of the late nineteenth century, they had allowed for feminine, sensual, and sexual forms and objects to enter into the highly rationalized, instrumental, and masculinized culture via the acceptable and "safe" register of "foreign souvenirs and fetishes" from cultures seen as inferior, feminized, and non-Enlightened by the day's authorities. The objects were generally seen to represent European humanity's uncivilized past, a past in which the realm of the physical and sensual was fully integrated with, as Comte put it, "a great and necessary stage in the theological development of humanity."[8] In this past, the power of those sensual objects coincided with the nineteenth-century power of commodity objects, which linked for consumers the commodities' emerging tactic of "the new" with the desire for an embodied encounter with the exotic.

The adaptation and practice of fetishism, encouraged by the insertion of African cultural objects, seems to be destined by the constricted and repressed shape of the emerging European—and particularly the French—culture of the late nineteenth century. It was a moment in which cultures collided and, despite the best efforts of an array of medical and psychiatric experts, new forms and considerations of objects were developed through the demands of desire:

That "primitive state" of wish-fulfillment is how Europe conceives of African thought: as a free reign of fulfilled desire, a place "to linger delighted" with the gods, where dualities of representation have been abolished in a single "fetish-religion," where ornamentation and physique coincide, where the alien native cries welcome in your own language, where the people are nothing but a "soft wax," and where "any figure that you wish" can be realized.[9]

Late nineteenth-century France was the most predictable location for this first great iteration, especially in view of the future great iteration in the late twentieth century. It was the most fertile place and the most receptive moment for this particular formation. Certain radical and cultural transformative developments converged at that time, when the unsettled political and philosophical landscapes provided the proper environment for radically subversive practices to emerge. It was, as Pietz puts it, "a cross-cultural situation formed by the ongoing encounter of the value codes of radically different social orders . . . one might say that the fetish is situated in the space of cultural revolution, as the place where the truth of the object *as* fetish is revealed."[10] And indeed, it is in the spaces of social revolution—or, as Foucault might suggest, in the great rupture—that the dying-but-still-limping classical cultures of Renaissance Europe encountered the modernist episteme, and later that modernist culture, having reached the same dry, empty spot, transformed into postmodernism.

On the one hand, many philosophers and historians in the late nineteenth century were still responding to the fetish as Comte did, as a religious object that indicated a part of the "great and necessary stage in the theological development of humanity."[11] The use of fetish objects was seen as man's attempt to negotiate with deities in order to fulfill his desires, through a tactic of totemism and idolatry. However, with the development of several distinct discourses in fin de siècle France—through the medical and psychiatric institutions and communities, the work of Sigmund Freud on sexual development, the French political situations that illuminated and foregrounded troubling developments in population concerns and therefore the various supposed "degenerative" practices of the French people, and the emerging feminist discourse that erupted with innovations in fashion and technology (the bicycle, chromolithography and therefore publishing of various forms)—all began to transform the *fetish* into a complex of cultural and sexual explanations and practices with profound implications for France, for modern cultures, and for fashion. To approach this network of conditions and iterations, we begin with a panoramic view of France in the latter part of the nineteenth century.

This age in France is marked by a convergence of social and cultural elements that we now condense into the period known as the fin de siècle. In retrospect, it signals a notion of Paris as an exotic, erotic place of sexual freedom, eccentric and elaborate fashions, symbolist poets, and innovative painters, and, despite current moral conditions, extreme decadence. The fin de siècle, in fact, marked an enormous upheaval in European culture, which was brought to bear via the pressures of increasing industrialism, commercialism, consumerism, the rise of the bourgeoisie, the decline of the aristocracy, and the emerging medical and psychiatric movements in France. This "rupture" between changing epistemes—between the great cultural confines of history—was marked by specific cultural attitudes and philosophies. It is indeed a rupture: a violent tear in the fabric of lived experience, manifested by radical changes in behaviors, attitudes, and fashions.

Fin de siècle France is precisely this sort of instance. Politically, France was still reeling from a humiliating defeat—both politically and militarily—in the 1870 battle of Sedan, ending the Second Empire with the capture of the main French army, the imprisonment of the emperor, and the establishment of the Third French Republic.[12] The civil unrest culminating with the Commune of 1871 gave a sense of impending chaos and violence to French citizens. In addition, a precipitous drop in birthrate in France at the same time that Germany was experiencing a rise in population brought alarm and concern in regard to the future safety of the nation.

In this unsettled atmosphere, the rise of the department stores—such as Bon Marché and Louvre (not to be confused with the museum of the same name)—brought an emergent middle class into prominence with its commercial interests and conservative politics. It also created an atmosphere of excitement and consumerist enthusiasm for the "latest fashions" with the innovation of Charles Worth and the couturier system, as well as the women's magazine, which brought fashion to a broader swath of the society: "[T]he old, rigid society-mould was visibly breaking up, with South African millionaires and other *nouveaux riches* storming the citadels of the aristocracy."[13] And this particular set of conditions made for an increasing prosperity, a democratizing of class distinctions, new opportunities for social mobility, and, with the Exposition, crowds of foreigners all attracted by the edgy beauty and nightlife of Paris.

Fetish, Fashion, and the Emergence into the Mainstream

In chapter 2, "Fetish Style History," we will traverse these complex lines of connection and association via the two great moments of iteration that are placed historically almost exactly 100 years apart. Each line of study will uncover the wildly diverse cultural events, developments, and subjects in these late decades of two centuries. In the First Iteration—perhaps unique in history for all its massive changes and contradictory implications and outcomes—France was the leader of the Western world in fashion. Though it borrowed much initially from Britain, which was previously the capital of fashion, the paradoxical indications and culture France developed became responsible for much of what has occurred in fashion and in fetish since then. The chapter will recognize and trace the myriad uncanny incidents and episodes of fashion and fetish emergent in French culture at the time and hopefully braid them together to form a comprehensible discourse: those strands represent, among other aspects, the medical/psychiatric texts, the saucy confrontational young women of the

Chérette posters of Alphonse Chéret, the emerging consumerism brought about by the invention of the department store, the rise of the couturier, the adaptation of the uniform for men of the *habit noir*, the political and cultural turmoil of the fall of the aristocracy and the rise of the bourgeoisie, the colonial imports from Africa and Asia, and the changing position of women in France.

In the Second Iteration, the period covering much of what many readers will be able to actually remember, we look at a second great time of rupture and transformation now commonly understood as the "postmodern turn." In this the tenets of modernism seemed to take a 180-degree about-face in its philosophies and practices, but principally in its shattering of gender roles and rules and its albeit grudging admission of previously forbidden Others—homosexuals, transsexuals, intersexuals, androgynies—and their underground practices, operations, and procedures. The process began in the postwar period of breaking social change in the 1960s with the hippie fashions. Both the genders rejected the extreme modernist and gendered fashions of the couture houses for the ragtag beaded, furred, and tie-dyed panoply of historic hand-me-downs worn by both genders and topped with either a massive Afro or long, loose, and sometimes dirty strands of hair, all existing, as the myth goes, in a fog of marijuana smoke. The emergence of punk in Britain was brought on by economic woes, the fashion wars fought between the Mods and the Rockers, and the brilliant introduction of fetish fashions merged with vintage clothes of designers Vivienne Westwood and Malcolm McLaren. Punk later expanded to the United States and other countries within the 1980s, helped along by Madonna's outrageous introduction of fetish fashions in her landmark book *Sex*; all the visible signs of the massive cultural transformations were occurring globally. By the 1990s, the couturiers had caught on and their fashion shows had become, as Caroline Evans suggests, a display of elaborate extremes and shocking evocations of death and decay. Further, the breathtakingly rapid advances of technological computing and media objects bring, in the first years of the new century, a new form of the dandy: the Nerd-Boy man (think a young Elvis Costello). With his adolescent-male gender re-established as the privileged subject, once again, young women were degenerated to their position as reproductive object for male consumption: a sad profile of sexual/reproductive availability marked by the then ubiquitous bare muffin-top abdomen and thong-revealing fashions of the "Girls Gone Wild" generation. All of these rapid transformations in fashion were the outward signs of radical, disrupting change that fetishized various characters who became the safety guides in the boundary crossings for the emerging postmodern culture.

Chapter 3, "Fetish Identity," tracks the emergence and development of new theoretical discourses around fetish, fashion, and their origins and complicated consequences during the seminal moments of the postmodern episteme, using theorists such as William Pietz, Emily Apter, Ulrich Lehmann, Anne McClintock, Judith Butler, Laura Mulvey, Joan Copjec, Mary Ann Doane, and Amanda Fernbach. Questions abound in this most important and essential aspect of culture, which, paradoxically, we as a culture are leery of facing, knowing that we will find it disturbing and perverse, with a vague sense of guilt. The essential and yet admittedly peculiar issue examined in this chapter is why the humble underwear of nineteenth-century women became, and has sustained, its position as the foundational basis for the fashions of fetish performance. This begins with the dominatrix but also exists in the succeeding fetish wear as it developed outward to emerge as fashion in terms of defining fabric and form when seduction and power are the goals.

It begins with the most obvious fetish practice of the nineteenth century, which continues in much the same fashion to the current time: cross-dressing, one of the first and perhaps most prevalent signs signifying the crisis in gender meanings in the late nineteenth century and now. It is examined through the prolific discourse that developed initially in the new form of mass media, the magazine, but was also found in medical journals, popular cultural graphic expressions, and the odd behaviors of certain individuals. Claiming it signified as the "figure that disrupts," Anne McClintock laces the practice of cross-dressing tightly into fashion: "Cross-dressing is not only a personal fetish, it is also a historical phenomenon. What one can call sumptuary panic [boundary panic over clothing] erupts most intensely during periods of social turbulence."[14]

Also discussed is the part played by the dandy—the late nineteenth-century "modern man" in his severe uniform of austerity and refinement. Stemming from the sporting culture of the time, he accentuates all the desired values of a modernist man of culture, though not as an aristocrat but as a "man of the people"; his Second Iteration copy is the nerd-boy of the late 1990s and early 2000s, whose regressive emergence also symbolizes the difficulties involved with giving up the power of his gender while immersed in a process of radical cultural change.

While men were sashaying about the culture as the modern ideal of rationality, somber responsibility, and power in the world of commerce and politics, women of the late nineteenth century were still dressed in the passé clothing of the previous era—the rococo. Powdered, bejeweled, and positioned in the center of dense layers of petticoats, skirts, and trim, woman resembled the symbol of the rose, signified as the reproductive organ (object) of the species, and was embedded in layers of richly colored and expensive fabrics, ribbons, and lace to attract a potential mate. And it is in that nineteenth-century juxtaposition—of subject as exclusively male and object as an abundance of possessions for which the female as domestic possession was but one—that we begin to unravel the complexities of the cross-dressing phenomenon. It becomes a hunt for the elusive phallus: imaginative symbol of masculine power and control, negotiated through the social and erotic politics of the culture through—strangely—fashion and costume. The scene was set in the boudoir, which becomes the underground theater of the domestic landscape, creating a flurry of fantasies illustrated in the arts of the time wherein the masculine becomes conflated with the feminine through an alchemy of drama and desire. Judith Butler identifies this paradoxical drama as a play of gender-as-performance that is not derived from natural sources but constructed entirely of precisely these sorts of cultural imperatives.

Finally, an essay by Laura Mulvey, "Some Thoughts on Theories of Fetishism in the Context of Contemporary Culture," assists in diagnosing the various theories—primarily of Marx and Freud—and explaining how we can understand and revise them for the contemporary era. She uses cinema to explain the "rich sight" that also works as an essential aspect of the fetish performance, whether in private or in the "public" performances in fetish clubs. Her essay provides a foundation for the further implications of the rich sight regarding the particular postmodern fashion transformations that are repetitive pastiches of fetish forms in an almost desperate iteration of difference and death.

Chapter 4, "Fetish Style: Fetish as Fashion," introduces the fashion corporations associated with famous fetish clubs that emerged from the underground to occupy large Internet sites showcasing and selling fashions used by fetishists. House of Harlot, Marquis, Demask, AMF, and other smaller concerns began selling fetish wear to the world through the Internet as fetish fashion at last emerged from the cultural closet. The chapter then reveals and discusses fetish fashions that have been organized via their effect on the body and identity of the fetishist through three key indications of pleasure and desire: *constriction*, *character*, and *effectuation*. My principal sources were the remarkable Mistress Jean Bardot[15] and the wonderful fetish community I encountered at the Ground Zero Club[16] in Minneapolis, Minnesota. I interviewed many participants with various fetish desires—dominatrices, tramplists,[17] slaves, transvestites, transsexuals, shoe fetishists, erotic asphyxiationists, and masochists who opened up to this "vanilla"[18] academic with such warmth and grace over a period of two years. They shared their background in fetish costumes and the sensations they experienced with rich detail and frankness.

Also, a lengthy interview with Mistress Jean Bardot—long an accomplished and insightful observer of human sexual behavior—in which she discussed her observations of the fetish effects and aspects of both the costumes and the narratives associated with them, led me to specify the three primary categories to showcase the ramifications of power and potency created by fetish costumes and performances. Though these categories refer to a primary action in play, virtually all fetish costumes are an amalgamation of multiple categories. I created the categories, however, as a way to manage the various quirks and qualities manifested by fetish costumes and thus as a way to discuss them.

Constriction describes the operating physical function for most of the fetish costume objects. But it also infers one of the primary cultural and perhaps psychological aspects of fetish expression: that of the boundary slippage in societies under radical change resulting in what McClintock calls a "sumptuary panic." In both the late nineteenth and late twentieth centuries, it is a question primarily of gender and bodily instability—brought on by the rigid gender roles established at the beginning and the end of the modern period. In the late nineteenth century, it arose as the influx of change brought on by the bourgeois, industrial, corporate, and consumerist revolutions that manifested as the replacement for the class systems of the aristocratic regimes. The radical changes brought on by identity politics and an extreme acceleration of technological mass communication that eluded authoritarian control by any forces other than public and transnational popularity caused the late twentieth-century rupture that emerged between the modern and postmodern epistemes.

Character is evocative of the narrative that many fetish practitioners require for satisfaction of desire. These narratives form around an originary experience of intense sexual feeling for the subject; to organize the chaos of sensations experienced, the mind puts the experience into a frame of reference that will allow the subject to understand its parameters and attempt to reproduce it again and again. As one informant explained to me, the original moment is so intense and confounding in its intensity that it ruins the now mundane pleasures of regular sexual experience. The fetishist, who has fetishized that narrative because of a now imaginary set of circumstances, is compelled to seek fulfillment from a fictive performance in which he is a character—the starring role—in a very precise drama. Oddly, many of the dramas seem to be linked in a collective set of narrativity, including a basis in S/M or sadomasochism, which has allowed the dominatrix to set up specific "sets" in her dungeon to facilitate these dramas (such as a medical room for the nurse/dominatrix to punish her submissive patient with the sharp tools of her trade). Because these performances are usually very specific to traditional feminine authority positions and settings in the "real" world, costumes for the dominatrix and the submissive are necessary to complete the illusion of the drama. Hence, costumes proliferate for nurse, governess, ringmaster, maid, cat-woman, military captain, and others that appear in the collections of such fetish fashion sites as House of Harlot, Torture Garden, Demask, AMF, and others. Most are constructed of rubber and have a minimal amount of ornamentation—just enough to secure the identity of the character—while the balance of the effect is the seductive revealing of the body of the dominatrix.

Finally, effectuation, which refers to a "bringing about of a certain effect," is a class of clothing in fetish performance that is used directly on the subject for gratification. This includes gloves, shoes, boots, whips, bondage straps and gear, gags, and masks that offer various accoutrements for actions on or into the subject. This is the most subversive and, frankly, the most disturbing category for most "vanilla" non-fetishists. Yet it is usually part of the S/M fetish performance and quite often part of fetish fashions and accessories. We tend to react to the degradation of the submissives in these narratives with disgust and horror. But it is because the male is so profoundly stationed as the strong authoritarian under the modernist regime that when we see the male submissive (they are usually but not always male) enduring and reveling in sexually explicit acts of degradation meted out by a dominant female, that we respond as the subjects of modern culture that we are: with repellant disgust. And this repellant disgust is precisely what the submissive—also a subject of modern culture—seeks. Yet once we take our hands away from our eyes and gaze upon these costume pieces, the gloss of horror disintegrates and curiosity begins. Thus understanding and acceptance begin their journey.

In chapter 5, "Fetish Style: Fashion as Fetish," we look at the surprising emergence of fetish signs in fashion designs from the couturier, the independent designer, and finally the fetish illustrator, who designs costumes in the realm of the imaginary and thus produces a costume that embraces the impossible and, consequently, the most desirable and most subversive of designs. But it was the work of the early adaptors of fetish fashion—beginning with the explosion of fetish signs that materialized in the shockingly overt but delightfully fun fashions of the club culture in the 1980s with the likes of Leigh Bowery, Boy George, and Madonna—that fetish truly enters fashion as part of the vast vocabulary of fashion forms. By the late 1980s, first Vivienne Westwood and later Alexander McQueen and other radical young, up-and-coming couturiers were regularly using fetish articulations in their collections. Fashion itself became fetishized by emerging DIY (do-it-yourself) young designers and design critics, who by the early twenty-first century were placing these fashions and critiques on the Internet through blogs and venues such as Etsy. Independent designers also appeared, broadening the practice of fashion design and merchandizing.

The various fetish signs and functions found in the fetish fashions that increasingly appeared in the work of these couturiers of the late twentieth and early twenty-first centuries will be examined for their manifestations, their presumed meanings, and their allure. But also, the fashion show (the performative aspect of fashion)—like the fetish show—animates and enlivens the fashion concept and articulates the "style" of the fashion through the dramatic narrative it uses as a context for the collection. Oddly, the fetish performance and the runway show of the couturier are merging in terms of style and narrative in the early twenty-first century. Both events, emerging from the same cultural context, begin to become more mainstreamed through the innovation of the Internet and, hence, become accessible to audiences who ordinarily would never experience such sights. Lehmann notes, "Fashion strives for an ideal, an abstract quality in itself. Fashion . . . always denotes the imaginary and nonexistent or sets the existing in contrast to the ideal."[19] The promulgation of that ideal has altered national and religious difference in dress and allowed for confrontations over items of clothing to become international conflicts.

Also in this chapter, the rupture in cultural formations is observed in the mannerist stylistic formations that have become the tactic of designers: through a carnivalization and parody of historic styles; a metamorphosis of histories, genders, class, and even species; and instability, intertextuality, fragmentation, and chaos. The opulence and extreme fetishistic character types that constellate in many fashion shows bring the shock of beauty, sex, and violence—the S/M triumvirate—to the public consciousness through panoramic visions that at once look old but are new, a sort of *trompe l'oeil* that fools us "by playing on what is and what seems to be in a labyrinth of interrelating self-conscious citations."[20]

Finally, in considering the future in chapter 6, we reach an apotheosis when encountering the ironic and paradoxical formations of fetish and fashion relationships, with their intertwined functions and similar goals. From the listing of possible futures, we posit as the most powerful a promise of agency, one of potential liberation through the expansion and play of identity formations that currently fuel the rapidly expanding costume play revolution. The notion of a performative *transversality*—a term gleaned from the discoveries of Félix Guattari on group dynamics—allows for the flow of imagined identities, sustains and enriches the individual subject through group recognition and interplay, and acknowledges the validity of multiple identities that may be expressed. It is a tactic that seeks to articulate the liberatory potential that can be observed residing in costume play. Its potential is found in the subject's relief from the restrictive conditions of the body, class, status, race, gender, and the culture that has always bestowed layers of repressive identities, restrictions, and codes onto the subject, who manifests the signs that rank the subject as "subject." When the subject releases the potential of multiple identities by acting in costume in community, he or she experiences a space of freedom away from the dominant cultural confines, which allows desires to flow freely and expression to expand through the consequent, stunning recognition that all identities are fictive identities. With that recognition, the bondage of accepted cultural positions and identities is also made fictive, and the subject experiences relief; in the shared relief of community comes the long-sought recognition of the subject as well as the subject's validity as a human being of worth. This most yearned-for of consequences seems utopian but is also within the realm of the possible.

Fetish Style History

[T]his emphasis on remembrance is inseparable from the sartorial. The rapidity with which the impressions of nineteenth century progress successively forced themselves on the artist were countered by using its most contemporary expression, fashion, to refer back to the past and create a standstill (as Benjamin notes) that appears far from conservative or retrospective, instead in its transhistorical potential it becomes a genuine paradigm of modernity.

Ulrich Lehmann[1]

In approaching the historical roots and promulgation of fetish and its effects on fashion—and vice versa—we will of course begin chronologically with what I refer to as the First Iteration, the late nineteenth century, and follow its progress to its most recent flowering in the late twentieth and early twenty-first centuries. But this is not to say that fetish did not exist before this period. I believe, even more firmly after this research, that the human relation to objects has always involved certain fetishistic attachments. But the fact is that within these two particular moments in history, under very particular circumstances that range across all aspects of human culture, this rich, perversely captivating, and puzzling type of theater formed around the conjoining of a sexual and an aesthetic relationship with objects. The stunning result has made this structural formation stand out as a compelling and increasingly important part of modern history. Though this particular formation begins as a product of Western cultures, by the contemporary period and through the expansive global reach of the Internet and other technologies of the late twentieth century, the Eastern cultures have not only assimilated the discourse on fashion and fetish, but have greatly enriched and enhanced it.

This chapter will begin by untying the tightly braided history of the late nineteenth century through its intertwined cultural innovations emerging from its technological and economic peculiarities. Much of the research on this period is covered by Valerie Steele, Ulrich Lehmann, Emily Apter, Anne McClintock, and William Pietz; yet this tale cannot be told to its fullest extent without identifying the cultural events that led inevitably to the flowering of the fetish/fashion iteration in the late twentieth and early twenty-first centuries. It extends directly from the First Iteration: its fashions, fetishes, and performances, though expressed through the cultural materials of our time, still bear the heavy trace of the previous century though its narratives, characters, and performances.

The First Great Iteration: Paris (1870–1900)

The Emerging Psychiatric and Medical Categorizations of Moral Behavior

Robert Nye in his essay on the medical origins of sexual fetishism[2] begins weaving together this convergence from late nineteenth-century France to form our contemporary notion of the definitions, objects, and practices of fetishism. This First Iteration takes place principally in France and especially in Paris. With a weakened government, France found itself in a self-conscious nationalistic dither concerning the slow adaption to new forms of production and industrialization and new constructions of society and class. But worse yet was an increasing awareness that they lagged behind other more prosperous and prepared nations—primarily Germany—since the "geopolitical status of the nation underwent a steady deterioration during this era, from the undisputed primacy under Napoleon I to the position of a second-rate power following the ignominious defeat at the hands of Prussia in 1870."[3] Not only was France behind in terms of economy and industrialization, but they were also experiencing a much lower birthrate.

This single issue had profound effects on the scientific, psychiatric, and medical developments in France in the latter half of the century. As Nye has noted, there were two principal concerns: first, in addition to the lower birthrate that indicated a future with fewer workers to bolster their flagging economy, and fewer natural resources, was the prospect that "by 1910 Germany would be able to put two soldiers in the field for every Frenchman . . . [which] exposed France to future dismemberment at the hands of its more aggressive and fertile neighbors."[4] But also, and more significantly, it fanned a firestorm of fears concerning impotency, criminality, and insanity centered around the medical concept of *degeneration*[5]—a concept that suggested depopulation may be evidence of the existence of a "hereditary stain" of weakness of mind and body that would inevitably lead to sterility. Rationalizing this fear was the notion developed by the newly formed medical authorities that this so-called degeneracy had infected the masculine drive to reproduce and further, though ironically, that excessive sexual activity was a key force in this depletion of desire. The culprit was masturbation, which drained the apparently limited potential of what they referred to as the "genital instincts" of both men and women, but women—being more "instinctual" and "biologically primitive"—did not deplete themselves as much as males, who also were depleted by their exercise of reason.[6]

It is in this peculiar consideration that the contemporary understandings of the fetish began to emerge. It becomes a founding text in which the suggestion is raised that objects that were the subject of obsessional sexual fixations could so pervert the attentions of the male that he would not be able to respond to the "proper object."[7] This condition was referred to as "erotomania" in *Des maladies mentales* (1838) by Etienne Esquirol, for whom the solution—the cure—was to be found only in a "moral treatment," through a dose of "mental reasoning." That "proper object" was of course the wife in a marital relationship with children as the result of desire, and it was only through a moral restructuring toward the "family" would the male recover his drive. The choice of "objects" determined male desire and perversion in the latter nineteenth century, and through the emerging authority of the medical and psychiatric professions, this would coalesce into a theory of fetishism that much later became, for Foucault, the "master perversion."

In 1882, French psychiatrists Jean-Martin Charcot and Valentin Magnan presented a landmark paper entitled *Inversion du sens génital*. The term *inversion* meant "homosexuality" in this period, and this paper presented the thesis that though there seem to be different sorts of "illnesses," in addition to homosexuality, all were in fact simply variations of the founding condition of degeneracy. Further, it posited that the other "different" perversions—what we have since come to know as the classical sexual fetishes concerning objects of clothing or textures—were the consequences of masturbation that "'weakened' the 'natural' instincts and opened the door to obsessive ideas."[8] But several years later, the contemporary understanding of the term *fetish* became concretized in the work of Charcot's student Alfred Binet, *Fétichisme dans l'amour* (1887) in the journal *Revue philosophique*. Rather than aim his thesis at the individual illnesses or obsessions, Binet takes the long view and contrasts these practices against the complicated cultural conditions of French culture in the 1880s—the "cultural crisis and exhaustion" of fin de siècle France. His basic thesis contended that

> all love was to some extent fetishistic, but . . . maintained that a kind of "psychic impotence" was invariably associated with the obsessive attention fetishists paid to a particular feature of the loved one or an article of clothing, or, worse still, an unrelated object . . . [and this was consequently] a "perverse predisposition" . . . the "characteristic fact" of fetishism . . . that heredity itself could not explain the particular attachment . . . for the origins of an individual fetish harkened back to some accident in the victim's psychic past.[9]

Several points become key in this statement: first, Binet uses the term *fetish* to refer to a practice of a sexual—rather than religious—attachment to the object. He also identifies the realm of the objects, particularly of clothing (the various items that become the essential taxonomy of fetish fashions, characters, and textures); and finally, he locates the "perverse predisposition" to an original "accident" that supposedly occurred in the psychic past of the practitioner. In fact, Binet also considered homosexuality as a fetish, saying that the only difference between them was in the "variation of life experience" that had precipitated this particular obsession. Although prior to this work various psychiatrists and doctors had moved the concept of the fetish from its early definition as a colonial religious object toward a transformation into a sexual object, it is Binet who finally gives the phenomenon a name, a cause, and a taxonomy of objects in a singular defining work.

Freud's later but profound contribution to fetishism accompanies a flurry of other famous works on sexology emerging at the time: in particular, *Psychopathia sexualis* (1886) by Richard von Krafft-Ebing and *Studies in the Psychology of Sex* (1897–1910) by Havelock Ellis. Freud published his *Three Essays on the Theory of Sexuality* in 1905. According to Nye, Freud's work tends to follow the prevailing theory of the French psychiatrists, that male impotence was caused by masturbation, which if not stopped could cause the patient to "be displaced along another path,"[10] the path of sexual deviation and neurosis. However, his insight was to "identify the libido as a sexual force that was neutral with respect to aim and object until fixed by a combination of the individual's life history and constitutional make-up."[11] In his essays, Freud laid out a landscape of sexual aberrations that he divided into categories of *object* and *sexual aim*. He discussed inversion—or homosexuality—under the first category of object. Fetishism was listed under sexual aim (the norm being heterosexuality), but he acknowledged that it could just as well be placed in the category of object, which would be seen from a contemporary view to be the most salient. It is an interesting development: in fetishism, Freud conflates aim and object, weakening his theoretical structure, yet in the end he posits that the relationship between the sexual instinct or constitution of the subject and the object of his attention needs to be "loosened" and reexamined. In his final works on fetishism, he rejects the prevailing theories of the French psychiatric and medical institutions to create his own theory of the castration complex, which unites "a powerful analytic matrix of symptoms, mental disturbances, and neurosis"[12] with the unified theory of psychosexual development in human beings.

Nye observes that these writings in this period—on both the sexual identity and the sexual perversion—are very similar in their approaches to the technical writings of the time. He notes that a recurring theme of the "strong woman/weak man" follows a general complaint and sense of resignation among male authors of the period toward the increasing emancipatory movements of women in various aspects of life, the suffragette protests being the most visible of these. But he also notes that a certain strain of literature featured women as objects described in terms of a masculine body ("supple body, sinewy legs, muscles of steel, and arms of iron"[13]) and, through an imaginary but absolute cultural acceptance of the gender binary, the feminization of the male protagonist. These works were seen as symptomatic of the moral and social decay of fin de siècle France but also reveal the profound effects from the insertion of strong female images into the culture of this period that so easily eroded the male psyche and his institutions.

The Position of Women in Fin de Siècle France

France was one of the last European countries to grant women the vote. In 1944, Charles De Gaulle enfranchised women as a wartime decree. In the late nineteenth century, action had started toward women's rights. Women bucked adverse opinions of the Left in France, which feared that women—in "their ignorance"—would vote for conservatives, and from the Roman Catholic Church, which believed such rights would emancipate women and lead them to abandon their families.[14] The salon contributed to women's growing political and cultural influence in the Paris of the late nineteenth century, promoting discussion of contemporary events and thinking among both men and women who attended these salons. It opened the intellectual potentials of women who had been sequestered in the domestic zone to a larger world, increasing their interests in education and suffrage. During the French Revolution, Marquis de Condorcet had spoken in favor of women's suffrage, and after the Revolution, women created political clubs and organizations that established a foundation for the movement to emerge.

The central concern for feminists in this period was a pervasive, toxic hegemony of masculine authority and control referred to as *masculinisme*.[15] Women in France were severely excluded from politics, higher education, and legal and other professions; and even where such exclusion did not exist, such as the home and factory, women were confined to profoundly subordinate positions. This situation was prompted by a key tenet under *masculinisme* that held that women had only one place and function—as mothers and teachers in the home: "In thus presuming a fundamental link between social role and innate characteristics, *masculinisme* resembled nothing so much as a form of racism in which the presence of female genitalia prefigured a common, unindividualized social destiny for half a population."[16] This constriction was punitively legalized and promulgated by the Napoleonic Code of 1804—a "'Paper Bastille' of legal restrictions"[17] that excluded and restricted the lives of women to the home under the total authority of husband and father: "Woman belongs to man, Napoleon maintained, as the tree and its fruit belong to the gardener."[18]

The Catholic Church also abetted the *masculinisme* ideology with its emphasis on women as "naturally" domestic and the innate and "weaker" predilections of women that required her subordination to the "reasoned" authority of the father or husband. The Church was also brought into the education of women in 1850, when the Falloux Law allowed for the establishment of a system of primary schools for girls. Though many communities refused to provide them, where they did come into existence, the Church exercised a predominant influence. In 1880, however, legislation created a secondary education for girls; in 1881, another law created a normal school for educating female secondary teachers; and finally in 1882, elementary education became compulsory.[19] With each succeeding advance, the influence of the church diminished, and public education revealed the discrepancies of the education of women in France.

Yet more revealing among *masculinisme*'s myriad profound restrictions to the body and soul of women, and certainly in terms of the formation of fetish in fashion, is what Bidelman refers to as the restrictions to personal mobility—particularly as it concerned the rules of dress for women. In France at this time, it was against the law for women to wear pants. Only women whose work outside the home required pants to be worn as a safety concern could successfully petition for a permit to wear pants. The fashion of the day called for complex layers of underwear, corsets, petticoats, skirts, blouses, hats, and accessories that meant a highly constricted, though also highly visible, presence in the world. In other words, the clothing of the day was radically gendered, by law and by class, as the "elaborate and expensive costumery worn by women became visible icons of male prosperity and class status."[20] Within this regimental and highly restrictive social condition—a condition that encodes clothing as a very particular collection of signs of a femininity that was domesticated, subjugated, idle, and sentimental against a masculine costume that was coded as militaristic, rational, authoritative, and related to work in the world—"it is perhaps understandable that exceptional women sometimes adopted the male attire, despite the law, or employed male pseudonyms."[21] This is, of course, cross-dressing, as McClintock explains its position in fin de siècle France:

> Cross-dressing is not only a personal fetish, it is also a historical phenomenon . . . a sumptuary panic (boundary panic over clothing) [that] erupts most intensely during periods of social turbulence . . . These changes led to the promulgation of sumptuary laws all over Europe, restricting "the wearing of . . . certain . . . styles to members of particular social and economic classes, ranks or 'states.'" Clothing became central to the policing of social boundaries . . . for this reason, . . . the cross-dresser becomes invested with a potent and subversive power . . . the transvestite is "the figure that disrupts."[22]

This is the foundation of the fetishistic conception in terms of these sumptuary objects and their semiotics of class and gender. It is in the obsessive and ossified classifications of class and gender around these costumes that the term *fetish* gains its foothold in fin de siècle France, in that the performativity of fetish begins to refine and define a practice and a relationship to objects. Cross-dressing linked the fetish as a practice to a set of objects—to fashion—and formed a community. The obsession with clothing for women, which had opened the door for the fetishizing of clothing, had also provided women with an occupation in which not only were they allowed to participate, but which in fact provided the impetus for the new economic phenomenon: the department store.

The Establishment of Consumerism: Couture Fashion and Merchandizing

As with the concept of the fetish, the discovery of meanings behind the concept of consumption and consumerism is approached by examining the terms. Also, as with the term *fetish*, there is a cloud of negative associations with the accusation of *consumerism* and *consumption*, especially as it is usually presented—*mass consumption*. It seems to place societies in the position of takers rather than producers or makers. It is almost the opposite of creativity, self-sufficiency, and the other modern designations that societies liked to imagine themselves to be. It is part of the mythic notions of who we were—though as soon as we say this, we also must acknowledge our enjoyment and celebration of things. However, Hannah Arendt has posited that:

> These two definitions are contradictory, since consumption cannot be the opposite of production when the two form a reciprocal and interdependent cycle necessary to sustain life . . . further . . . that impermanent "consumer goods," having their purpose in the maintenance of life, should be distinguished from "use objects," intended to create a world of durable things as a familiar home for [hu]man in the midst of non-human nature . . . that . . . one [is] related to life sustenance, the other to giving meaning to life.[23]

This phenomenon coincides with the development in late nineteenth-century France of the department store; chromolithography (color lithography); the expansion and increased readership of newspapers, posters, and magazines; and the rise in advertising and its strategies. In other words, the proliferation and distribution of *things* and the compelling advertisements for *things*, as a result of the Industrial Revolution, meant a radical change in the way we began to understand what we needed and what we desired: that which was related to life sustenance, and that which—increasingly—gave meaning to life.

The rich cornucopia of things laid out for perusal in the large department stores of this era and the highly detailed and beautifully colored fashion plates, posters, and advertisements in newspapers and magazines began to create a desire to *see* these things: "The merchandise itself is by no means available to all, but the *vision* of a seemingly unlimited profusion of commodities is available, is, indeed, nearly unavoidable."[24] This visual opulence created a habit of desire—in the sense of an addiction—for seeing opulence and has had far-reaching implications for the fetish as a psychosexual development brought on not just by *seeing* plenty but by sensing an embodied *possibility*. Much of the extreme amount of pornography at this time was in fact evident in photographs seen in sidewalk stands of stereoscopic apparatuses, which for a small fee imposed a private sexual and sensual experience of opulence and possibility upon the viewer. The "visual priority of the object closest to the viewer and on the absence of any mediation between eye and image . . . was a fulfillment of what Walter Benjamin saw as central in the visual culture of modernity: 'Day by day the need becomes greater to take possession of the object—from the closest proximity—in an image and the reproduction of an image.'"[25]

Under these conditions, the French pioneered retailing and advertising strategies, the twin pillars of modern consumer life.[26] Before 1851, when the Great London Exposition altered attitudes concerning consumerism and marketing, advertisement was only minor effort. Poor-quality, text-heavy handbills, posters, and newspaper ads prevailed. But with the advent of photography and chromolithography, the image-based advertisement and poster became immediately and overwhelmingly popular with printers and public alike. Victorian graphic design focused on the emotional values of the emergent middle-class culture: sentimentality, patriotism, and a particularly cloying domesticity prevailed. By the 1890s, "advertizing had emerged as the central cultural form of commodity capitalism";[27] and it was also in this same wedge of time that France, and especially Paris, became the fashion center of the world. McClintock states that by this time, the commodity in general (and fashion specifically) had become such a profound cultural phenomenon that it also represented a new cultural system for distributing social values and status, not only in terms of clothing but in the vast proliferation of manufactured things. Further, this proliferation of things was also a proliferation of signs, in that the promotion of expositions, museums, and advertising created a spectator sport—"a panorama of surplus as spectacle."[28] Advertising begins to unlock the vigilantly guarded boundaries that marked the limits of the public and private, and of market strategies and spectator desires, making possible the profound conflation of desire and commodity that distinguishes the fetish relationship.

It is here that we begin to add another strand to the braid that is the history of the fetish. In France, there had been a revolution—not just in terms of new freedoms for women, but also in terms of the rise of couture and the growth of fashion media. This set of conditions is exemplified by the emergence of a popular cultural phenomenon: the "Chérette." In 1881, an old law in France severely restricting the censorship and the placement of posters in public was lifted, allowing the posting of images anywhere but churches, polls, or other sensitive areas.[29] This caused a massive expansion of magnificently colored, large-scale posters. The invention of chromolithography in 1837 meant prints were created in remarkably clear, detailed color with a dramatic intensity and great variation in hue. The faster, mechanized presses meant that posters and other printed material—including fashion plates—were produced rapidly and distributed to a broad market for less cost. Posters were immediately plastered across Paris, delivering their direct and uniquely powerful messages to the French public: "the streets became an art gallery for the nation."[30]

Jules Chéret, dubbed by critics as both the "father of the modern poster" and (less credibly) the "father of women's liberation,"[31] began in 1881 to create what is known as the "visual poster," in which the image is overwhelmingly the most powerful aspect of the communication. His posters were produced in sizes up to about two meters because he insisted on representing the women in his posters at approximately actual scale. Chéret had arrived at a modern conception of the poster composition: he had experimented with various elements and discovered that the most provocative composition was a simple yet striking design created through a painterly image of saturated colors and dynamic movement and a minimum of typography. The effect mythologized his subjects, the characters of the Parisian nightlife. The women in his posters, advertising the panoply of particularly domestic and feminine goods then available, were to have a profound effect on the emerging notions of the

Dans tous les Cafés

Fig. 2.1 Jules Chéret (1836–1932), untitled poster, c. 1900. The woman in the poster was emblematic of the "Chérette" style, displaying her independence and pluck. Photo courtesy of Buyenlarge/Getty Images.

emancipation of women. It was in his concept, design, and painting of these women that he made his most radical move. As Philip Meggs recounts,

> Options for women were limited, and the proper lady in the drawing room and the trollop in the bordello were stereotyped roles, when into this dichotomy swept the Chérettes. Neither prudes nor prostitutes, these self-assured, happy women seemed to be enjoying life to the fullest without any fear of disapproval or disgrace, wearing low-cut dresses, dancing, drinking wine, and even smoking in public.[32]

The allure of this image for both men and women—though with different effects—was profound. Represented by Chéret in many different versions for many different clients, the Chérette retained a very specific identity as an icon of confidence, joy, and self-assuredness that inspired women and was fetishized by men. Because of the massive popularity of this iconic fad, other poster artists picked up the practice. In the 1890s, as the art nouveau style developed in France, this image of the aggressively confident woman continued to proliferate as a key trait of art nouveau ornamentation and representation. However, in some works, she could take on a more sinister aspect and was usually represented in conjunction with the "natural world" of entwining plants, water, or insects, revealing a bit more of the apprehension of the potential obsessions and "natural instincts" with which women were associated.

The "Latest Fashion"

This commercialization of fashion that Chéret's work illustrates began, however, in the making and marketing of popular trends in clothing and cosmetics with the advent of the Industrial Revolution in Britain in the eighteenth century. With the rise of the middle class or merchant class, whose desire for upward mobility and status created an interest in "the latest fashion," came the demands for marketing to increase sales and new communication outlets for advertising. New agents emerged in the spread of fashion intelligence: "the Manchester men, the Scotch Drapers, Scotch Hawkers and the provincial shopkeepers,"[33] but also the fashion plate, the fashion magazine, and the fashion doll. In the beginning of the eighteenth century, Paris had been the center of fashion for the elite and, as such, had annually sent out a "fashion doll"—a wooden mannequin—sometimes made to actual scale and dressed in full accoutrement: undergarments, dresses, accessories, and hairstyles. It was sent to European courts and particularly to Britain, as fashion was at this time the domain of the aristocracy alone. Once the British court had learned from it, it went to the shops and dressmakers and from there on to other places beyond London, achieving a great spread of influence but with little impact, given that the goods were too expensive for all but the most exclusive clientele.

In the last decade of the eighteenth century, the English arrived at a brilliant, if prosaic, solution that began to expand fashion as a mass consumer product: the paper doll of fashion. From 1790 on, the English fashion dolls—made of cardboard, about eight inches high, with many dresses, hats, underwear, chemises, corsets, and negligees, and all adjustable to suit the nuances of fashion—were shipped off in complete sets in an envelope to hundreds and later thousands of women to teach the details of what latest fashions signaled "good taste." Eventually, different sets were produced to appeal to women of various classes and professions.[34] When discarded, they were handed to children, creating a new form of toy that delights even to this day but also beginning "the indoctrination of the next generation of fashion consumers—teaching even in infancy the importance and intricacies of fashion awareness." The paper doll was "so humble and so ephemeral as to be beneath the notice of most historians but [was] symptomatic of the rapid changes in the diffusion of fashion views."[35]

The first fashion magazine appeared in France in the 1670s, but it was again in England that the mass production of the fashion plates began. The first fashion print appears with the first fashion advertisements in *The Lady's Magazine* in 1770.[36] By the following year, the first hand-colored print appeared—and immediately expanded in circulation. These offered a visual lushness for women to gaze upon, allowing for the whiff of a fashionable embodied potential for women. George Lukács locates this potential in the commodity as a central pivot between culture and commerce, joining the confluence of art and money, aesthetics, and economy.[37] Certainly the "fashion plate"—a term that came to mean literally "a person who dresses fashionably"—figures precisely as a junction between these cultural practices and concerns, a position that began in the eighteenth century but by the late nineteenth century became highly explicit. These new tactics culminated in the advent of the mass production of the *notion of fashion*. Building desire in the readers and consumers of these objects led to an ever-increasing market of people of all classes through expanding colonization and commodification of the emerging fashion industry and the consuming visual experience of advertising. That desire is constructed around the visual consumption of spectacle, on the consumption of fantasy. The fantasy begins to suggest its own landscape of potential, a place in which the image reflected back to the viewer offers an identity of embodied splendor of class, and with it, exclusivity as a fashionable, unique identity. Thus, becoming fashionable meant the alleviation from the confines of class: in essence, it meant achieving a sort of *para-class* of taste, rather than economic or social rank, as a potential identity. McClintock described the distinction as a shift "from the axis of possession to the axis of spectacle," in that actual possession of fashionable clothing was no longer necessary to produce a space in which the subject could experience the landscape of upper-class taste and fashion: "[B]y manipulating the semiotic space around the commodity, the unconscious as a public space could also be manipulated." Advertising began to understand how, through manipulation of texts and images using "subterranean flows of desire and taboo," it could redirect the public toward "buying class."[38]

The nature of that experience is described as a fantasy of class mobility: Whether it actually entails the wearing of fashionable clothes or, more subversively, playing with paper dolls, the assumption of an awareness of the fashionable introduces (through the visual consumption of images) the experience of plenty, of luxury, and of refinement that satisfies at the same time it also reinstates desire. Once fashion plates were mass-produced as advertising, they resulted in a highly improved vision of high fashion viewed through a distinctly middle-class understanding of the women of fashion: "Fashion was the key used by many commentators to explain the forces of social imitation, social emulation, class competition, and emulative spending. They were the motive forces which made fashion such a potent commercial weapon."[39] Although it was actually beer that arguably became the first truly mass consumer product, nevertheless, fashion becomes the consumer product that draws the attention of contemporary critics of the changing social and cultural scene. Dress as a signifier of class and social position in the late nineteenth century becomes blurred by the increasing availability of inexpensive, mass-produced clothes based on the fashions of the elite. Critics lamented the loss of exclusivity in terms of their identity: no longer was their identity as upper class distinctively visible from their clothing. An eighteenth-century critic complained, "[T]his rage for finery and fashion spreads from the highest to the lowest; and in public places . . . it is very difficult to guess at [people's] rank in society or at the heaviness of their purse."[40]

Fashion as Modernity's Pillar

Of all the cultural ingredients that came to a boil in the late nineteenth century creating the definition and practice we now understand as fetish, it is the emergence of the notion of fashion, as we have seen, that is the most pertinent and most essential element. *Fashion* has an extensive definition—as prevailing style, a manner of making, an industry—and a concept of *the new* pervades and overarches all definitions and practices that appear under fashion's expanding influence. Yet although fashion is defined by the new, it is also always redolent with the past, as most scholars understand and, indeed, as becomes obvious once examined closely. As Ulrich Lehmann states,

> The characteristics of high fashion were established at the origin of modernity, the latter half of the nineteenth century. Subsequent sartorial avant-gardes are always already *passéiste*. That is . . . fashion has to mark absolute novelty yet has already died when it appears in the physical world . . . In order to become new, fashion always cites the old—not simply the ancient or classical, but their reflection within its own sartorial past.[41]

This is to say, "the new" is necessarily a consideration of, or a reaction to, past styles and practices. Fashion, in particular, is defined through its search for novelty via its past presence. Any individual past a certain age who is conscious of fashion will begin to recognize a circularity in the frequency at which particular sartorial details, forms, and concepts begin to reappear in fashions presented as "the latest thing." Fashions that begin from the late nineteenth century on are associated with and, even more so, begin to define modernity. Yet even as fashion defines modernity, "without the connotation of antiquity, modernity loses its raison d'etre—its adversary and point of friction, which is also its stimulant."[42]

By the eighteenth century, the Marquis de Caraccioli exclaims, "To be in Paris without seeing the fashions, you have to close your eyes. The scenes, streets, shops, carriages, clothing, people, everything presents only that . . . They want new fabrics . . . modern systems."[43] In 1868, partially in recognition of France's grow-ing economic status and identification with fashion, but also perhaps in a move to secure class boundaries, the Chambre Syndicale de la Haute Couture was formed to "police" the booming couture industry and to draw a distinction between the com-mon dressmaker/tailor and the couturier. The dressmaker and tailor merely copied or improvised clothing based on the fashions seen in either illustrations in the fashion magazines or the fashion dolls, whereas the couturiers were designers; they created new or innovative designs that were the particular purview of the upper classes. Although Charles Worth is considered the first couturier, Rose Bertin was in the late eighteenth century an early prototype of the couturier with her designation as a *marchande des modes*, which initially referred to someone who added trim to gowns, but by 1776 had been redefined as "dressmaker." Bertin was a highly cre-ative designer with a distinctive personality and an elevated sense of her class and consequently became a model for the couturiers to come. Worth, working in Britain the 1850s, also cultivated a dramatic personality as a creative designer and had the distinction of being a "man in a profession dominated by women." Soon, there were a number of couturiers whose "houses" catered to the royal and the nouveau riche bourgeoisie, both further instantiating the class distinctions, yet also responding to and even furthering women's changing role. This designation as a *designer*, new to the lexicon of fashion, was promoted by the couture houses, which were in the business of developing what we would now refer to as a brand—a recognizable, distinctive style based on the couturier and his/her personality and social connec-tions, which the consumers of the time—women of the upper classes—felt conferred further status on them.[44]

The Habit Noir and the Great Renunciation

Although in contemporary times men's fashions coming from Paris couture and elsewhere can include all colors and all manner of free-form constructions, the basic men's suit remains the stalwart of men's apparel. Regardless of the many colors, fab-rics, cuts, and accessories of the contemporary men's suit, it remains formulaically stable as a uniform of modern, successful, mature masculinity. It was not always so: "For centuries men dressed as magnificently as women—and often more so—but al-ready at the beginning of modern fashion, we find hints of the great division that later separated the sober, very slowly changing male uniforms from bright and stylish female fashions. This distinct separation is known as 'the great renunciation.'"[45] Not only was the opportunity to dress in magnificent finery renounced, but the renuncia-tion reflected the deep crevasse that opened between the genders, which was to have drastic effects on both culture and couture.

Further, we can see the power relations that become invested in the clothing of the French kings and court of the time—especially that of Louis XIV—through its associations with the rituals of a fetishized etiquette surrounding the daily dressing of the king. He was, quite literally, the height of fashion. Dressing him in his layers of finery was a highly visible honor and part of the elaborate ceremony attached to his daily waking. The dressing of the king was a symbolic ritual performance of royal acknowledgment and daily reinstatement of rank as he quite literally (ad)dresses the kingdom with its nobility and social ranking. These most humble and private of tasks were, for the French court of the time, an exacting performance of privilege and rank that was reestablished daily, "a type of organization by which each act represented a rank position symbolizing the distribution of power."[46]

Norbert Elias, writing on etiquette and ceremony in court society, refers to this ritual as a "prestige-fetish," in that it was highly competitive, incredibly exacting in its detailed symbolic indications of rank and placement at court, and highly sought after by its members.[47] Desire for status and favor meant that this ritual became intensely scrutinized for minute details of performance that revolved around not only the king's highly fetishized clothing and gestures but also the reactions of the large audience accompanying each of these acts. Status, that is, one's relative social standing, and rank, one's official hierarchical standing in formal societal structures, both became intensely linked symbolically through the rigorous and exacting performance around the clothes and the dressing of the king. What he wore encouraged an increasing interest in men's fashion, and as a result, the "arbiter of elegance" emerged, often a favorite of the king, who would derive innovative fashion from the king's clothing. Fashion then trickled down from court to the nobility, but certain caveats, innovations, and taboos separated and fetishized what nobility could wear from that worn by the king, keeping his status and rank secure and, in so doing, securing the stability of the kingdom.

However, the British male fashions were not as florid and flamboyant as the French: by 1740, many men wore clothes similar in style to the working class, though with very high-quality stuffs. The improved quality of woolen cloth, the growing influence of Enlightenment philosophies, the rising bourgeoisie and libertarian movements in Europe, and early industrialization of textile and other industries fostered an emerging spirit of democratization and egalitarian thought in British society. Male fashions were simpler, less formal and decorative, and influenced by the sporting clothes worn by British aristocracy. British ideas of French styles were influenced by the long tension between the two nations. The French styles were seen—with a sniff of a British sense of superiority—as part of the French moral and social decline, as effeminate and weak. Thus, plainer male dress began to spread even into France, and the linkage between political and philosophical beliefs and the clothes one wore began to take on more emphasis, extending "from England to France in the 1770s and 1780s, as part of a wave of Anglomania that sometimes (but not always) implied an appreciation of English political liberties. The French *philosophes* had admired the liberal politics of England and the supposed virtuous simplicity of country life—both elements of which were at least implied by the English style of informal country dress."[48] But there was also much bantering back and forth about the virtues of the English style and the veracity of their "egalitarian profile" in the French press. Nationalism drove the discussion into patriotic invectives, yet there was an event that would eventually make this banter a moot point.

Entering this foray was a rather subversive yet "modern" male type: the dandy, whose aesthetic was instead—"in a Kantian sense—'disinterested.'"[49] Fashion had always been a statement of class, wealth, and status. George "Beau" Brummell (1778–1840), an English "man of fashion," was a bourgeois man whose occupation is sometimes listed as "socialite." His social success—reaching well beyond his own

Fig. 2.2 George Eastman (1854–1932), pictured in his *habit noir*, turned from banking to photography, producing a successful roll film in 1884 and the "Kodak" box camera in 1888. He formed the Eastman Kodak Company in 1892. Photo courtesy of SSPL/Getty Images.

class—was based on his storytelling ability and his quick wit. For Brummell, fashion was no longer a statement of class but a "moral code that declared the virtues of eschewing everything ostentatious and displaying individuality through well-chosen details rather than grand gestures."[50] He was at school with the Prince of Wales—the future George IV—who had taken to Brummel's wit and grace, calling him the "handsomest and pleasantest man of the age." Eventually, Brummel's attitudes and lack of funds reduced him to penury, but not before he had solidly established a radically new profile of modern masculinity. As Ian Kelly suggests, "The way men began to dress because of Brummell was an arresting corollary to the sea change in attitudes toward masculinity, and the debate over gentlemanly behavior that reverberates in the novels of Jane Austen as much as in the politics of the Enlightenment."[51] This new suit worn by Brummell consisted of a redingote[52] (based on a riding coat), gilet (similar to a long vest, buttoned up the front), and long tight-fitting trousers with stirrup straps called pantaloons. It was simple, elegant (or do we not think "elegant" because of the enculturation of these aesthetics learned since?), in soft neutral colors and particularly in black.

And what was this new profile of modern masculinity? Despite the upper-class company he kept, Brummell's radical costume—which became essentially a uniform—was ostensibly practical, simple yet elegant, and most importantly, symptomatic of the modern culture forming at the time: "it is a *habit* (in the literal sense of the word)."[53] This habit was critical of the overwhelming crass consumerism of the nineteenth century, yet in eschewing the consumerism of his time, he merely replaced it with a simpler model. But dandyism is not simply a costume; it is a lifestyle. A dandy "'should have a light, insolent, conquering air, take care over his toilette and wear moustaches' . . . [talk] only of horses, racing and carriages and scarcely [know] of the existence of women."[54] In adopting dandyism, the dandy becomes what was only a conjecture for Brummell, Jacques Vaché, Craven, Rigaut, and the other dandies: the truly modern man. Lehmann positions this radical change in attitudes toward the male profile as part of the aftershock of the French Revolution, when the fashion for male costume became restricted to small variations on a limited number of garments.

This limitation had become paradigmatic since "The 'Great Renunciation'—that is, the time after the French Revolution when the European male 'abandoned his claim to be considered beautiful. He henceforth aimed only at being useful.'"[55] The previously distinct sartorial codes of class and rank symbolized by male fashion became passé—and for some—a dangerous practice, replaced by the more democratic dark three-piece suit, or *habit noir*. Of course, there still were distinctions to be made and observed in the fabric, cut, and tailoring of the suits of the different classes, but the extremes previously found in these suits had melted away with the onset of modernist thought. Instead, the *habit noir* ostensibly symbolized a new individuality (despite the irony that the suit was and is worn by most men of all classes—literally a "uniform" of masculinity). Brummell framed his distinction by adhering to a conformist concoction of modern masculinity: to be elegant is to be inconspicuous, to blend in. And this is part of the chains of contradictions of Brummell: he is essentially suggesting blending in with the black suits of the vast working classes, who could not afford showy textiles of the previous French styles. Yet he insisted on his aristocratic and effete demands for immaculate linens and the best textiles and accessories.

Charles Baudelaire describes the dandy—or the *flâneur*, as his 1859 landmark essay "The Painter of Modern Life" titles him—as such:

> Dandyism does not even consist . . . in an immoderate taste for the toilet and material elegance . . . these things are no more than symbols of his aristocratic superiority of mind . . . the perfection of his toilet will consist in absolute simplicity . . . It is first and foremost the burning need to create for oneself a personal originality, bounded only by the limits of the proprieties. It is a kind of cult of the self . . . Dandyism is the last spark of heroism amid decadence.[56]

These calls for absolute simplicity, personal originality, and a cult of the self are certainly recognizable to a contemporary understanding of the ubiquitous modernist subject, down to its single-gendered designation. And even the seemingly paradoxical costume of the dandy as the *habit noir*—the black wool suit, "the dark attire of the nightly flâneur,"[57] serving as the sartorial mark of a "personal originality" that, in fact, all dandies wore—has become the ever-present, universal masculine dress suit of the modern era, the uniform of the established modern male.

This paradox is not a paradox if considered from the standpoint of the late nineteenth century: it is an originality not of the actual self but of a class, or more accurately of classless selves that required a code and a set of signifiers pointed toward a certain ideology that was just emerging from the hegemony of aristocratic fashion. Baudelaire positioned these men as "artists" in that they had opted out of the prevailing order and re-created themselves in opposition to the establishment, and he insisted, "Dandyism, an institution beyond the laws, itself has rigorous laws which all its subjects must strictly obey."[58] That law called out the long-adhered-to sartorial laws of class distinctions and adopted instead a uniform of "disinterest." The neutral-toned plain suit of the dandies provided a classless designation but at the same time established them as a particular sort of subject: "they all partake of the same characteristic quality of opposition and revolt; they are all representatives of what is finest in human pride, of that compelling need . . . of combating and destroying triviality."[59] As Lehmann suggests, it is "precisely sartorial fashion that establishes the depicted as a *social* being."[60]

The adoption of the suit—"the outer husk of the modern hero"[61]—which fomented the "Great Masculine Renunciation" of the right to be considered beautiful, thus positions the Victorian male in a very particular cast: uniformed in what becomes a specifically masculine signification with precious little leeway in terms of variation, individual subjects (despite their natural creativity and independence) become the universalized character of the "modern man." The *habit noir*, "which transcends time and style with its abstracted and invariable appearance,"[62] with its potent symbolic construction negates any deviance, nuance, or suggestion of the feminine. It is an absolutely pure representation of a masculinity that became utterly singular, empowered by its multiple meanings and the efficiency with which its ubiquitous form delivers the communication. The movement in men's fashions since the nineteenth century has been remarkably static. Yet the renunciation was not only in terms of beauty, but as Flügel suggests, it also was a renunciation of erotic display: "Hitherto man had vied with woman in the splendor of his garments, woman's only prerogative lying in *décolleté* and other forms of erotic display of the actual body; hence forward, to the present day [1930], woman was to enjoy the privilege of being the only possessor of beauty and magnificence, even in the purely sartorial sense."[63] He suggests that men after the French Revolution had to de-emphasize class and wealth for a "doctrine of the brotherhood of man"[64] and display dignity in the ideals of work, commerce, and industrialization. And with those heavy responsibilities came a change in "psychical inhibitions" and morality, with the result that

> modern man has a far sterner and more rigid conscience than has modern woman, and that man's morality tends to find expression in his clothes in a greater degree than is the case with women. Hence it is not surprising that . . . modern man's clothing abounds in features which symbolize his devotion to the principles of duty, of renunciation, and of self-control. The whole relatively "fixed" system of his clothing is, in fact, an outward and visible sign of the strictness of his adherence to the social code (though at the same time, through its phallic attributes, it symbolizes the most fundamental features of his sexual nature).[65]

Modern man's "sexual nature" therefore has become limited—perhaps it is more apt to say *sacrificed*—to signs of "duty, of renunciation, and of self-control," linking the notion of the *habit noir* paradoxically to the habit of nuns through its consistent black-and-white uniformity and self-flagellatory adherence to "duty."

As Lehmann suggests, this remarkably solid and durable modernist brotherhood of the *habit noir*—universally accepted even unto contemporary times—provided a backdrop for the "sartorial excesses of the feminine."[66] I would suggest that precisely this condition of sacrifice, strict adherence to social and commercial codes, and Victorian bourgeois morality—which "suits up" the masculine subject into a uniform of paternalistic power yet prescribes rigid rules of an absolute masculinity that so confined and humiliated men (for who would truly be up to such a profile?)—pushed these men to seek release in the subversive performance of fetish in the fashions of the feminine. And in so doing, they developed a taxonomy of fetish objects and clothing that has retained its power and influence on female fashion and in the performance of fetish to this day.

Layers of the Feminine: The Fashions of Females

At this point, we arrive at the final and, in some ways, the most significant strand of the braid: problematizing the feminine and female fashion in conjunction with the emerging concept of fetish as the organizing practice that envelops, condenses, and activates all the aspects in the discussion so far: the complex cultural history of France in the late nineteenth century. All of these conditions and contingencies were pulled into the vortex of the pivoting notion of fashion and fetish, and specifically feminine fashion, in fin de siècle France.

François Boucher emphatically states, "The most typical features of the development of costume in Europe from 1850 to 1868—the appearance of couture, technical improvements, economic expansion and the preponderance of French fashions—were all linked to a common factor, which in turn corresponds to a general characteristic of society: it was the ever-increasing rapidity of change."[67] Nor was it to slow up in the continuing period of the late nineteenth century; in fact, he demonstrates that the two factors that stand out in this period were evidence of rapid change: first, European fashion developed similarly in all parts of Europe, but also in the United States, Africa, and Asia because of the constant advancement of technical, commercial, and industrial expansion of both Europe and the United States. Secondly, in perhaps the first globalized expansion of the market, and despite certain national and cultural differences and distances, French fashion became the first global fashion to gain acceptance: "Therefore where this period is concerned, the history of costume is the history of costume in France."[68]

In this period, France in general but Paris specifically had developed a culture of elegance and sophistication in art, music, and theater. In post-revolutionary Paris, the social class system that privileged the aristocracy and upper middle class, though still somewhat intact, had broadened to include the actors, artists, and performers of the *demi-monde*, whose creative adaptations to fashion influenced further fashion design through the nightly parade of the latest fashions in the theater, in cafés, and on the avenues of Parisian nightlife. A mutually beneficial relationship developed among the actresses, the great ladies of Paris society, and the couturier that has lasted to the contemporary era: the appearance of the latest couture fashions worn by famous women creates a buzz and a desire for those fashions in the public.

Women's fashions had, with the exception of the empire and consulate periods early in the century, been following a particular sartorial profile: long full skirts, sometimes with layered flounces trimmed with ribbons, lace, or other forms of trim; the waist cinched in tightly from the corset that was the mainstay of Victorian costumes; which then broadened with Bertha collars, shawl-shaped collars, or leg-o-mutton sleeves. Collars either formed a graceful deep *décolleté* from the brow of the shoulder to just above the breast line or they were brought up tightly to the neck. Boucher suggests, "After 1821–2, transformations in costume corresponded to

Baroque, Rococo or Neo-Gothic movements in taste, bringing heavier, more expansive and solemn forms, popular particularly among the rich middle classes."[69]

However, by the middle of the century, the changes that were to revolutionize women's clothing and fashion, and create the forms that would become the fashions of fetishists, were at hand. When the department stores began selling women's clothing, the power valence of fashion began to expand, from the preferences of the wealthy buying from individual designers to the market forces of the middle and lower classes buying ready-to-wear clothing from department stores. The department stores were soon the primary source for clothing, providing the entire process of clothing design and merchandizing. And this new condition meant that now the commercial market would continue to change fashion:

> [F]ashion entered a new economic phase during the second half of the nineteenth century, the period of "high capitalism." The traditional production of clothing developed in two new directions: toward *grand couture* (the exclusive productions of the great dressmakers like Worth and Madame Paquin) and *confection* (the mass production of ready-made clothing).[70]

Women's fashion in terms of its "full-blown forms, overloaded ornament and strictly regulated ways of wearing clothes"[71] had remained essentially the same since the empire period. By the late nineteenth century, however, changes began to seep into styles. The women's emancipation movement, though arguably slower than elsewhere and only minimally successful in France at this time, nevertheless spawned considerations in fashion a bit more toward convenience and comfort. Also the development of "sport" as a recreational pastime necessitated a line of clothing types to accommodate participation. In 1848, an American, Amelia Bloomer, published a feminist journal based on the ideas generated by the first women's rights convention in Seneca Falls, New York. In 1851, *The Lily*—as it was called—began running articles on the necessity for clothing that allowed women to be more actively involved and thus established the notion of "bloomers," a style based on "Turkish" pantaloons,[72] for which the press of the time attached Bloomer's name. For feminists of the time, "[b]inding clothes were both a metaphor for the constricted position of women in society as well as a prime instrument in the control of women's lives."[73] The popularity of the bicycle in Paris had led to shorter skirts and what we would call culottes—a skirt divided and sewn together to form wide, billowing pants.

Further, Boucher suggests that the rapidly emerging art forms at this time—such as art nouveau, impressionism, and postimpressionism—that dominated all levels of fashionable Parisian culture also had a profound effect on the design and profile of women's fashion, attributing to them a less ornamented style and a gently curvaceous profile following the somewhat natural lines of the feminine form. Although aided by corsets and bustles, this profile represented a more "natural" form than the exaggerated hourglass lines of the earlier part of the century. Boucher suggests that from 1870 to 1905, costume design may have also been affected by the "materialism, sensuality and naturalism" of the literature of the period. The prevalent references to the writings of Proust, Baudelaire, Balzac, and others in the contemporary works on fashion history and analysis (which have made much of the constant and close descriptions of the characters' clothing in their novels and essays) validate Boucher's view. Proust, for example, discusses the dress of his heroine, Albertine, describing an art nouveau palette of "sleeves . . . of a Scottish plaid in soft colours, pink, pale blue, dull green, pigeon's breast, the effect was as though in a grey sky there had suddenly appeared a rainbow."[74]

Boucher submits that from the end of the Second Empire (1868) to the First World War (1914), the development of women's fashions underwent three distinct stages, the first two of which are relevant to this discussion. Regarding the first stage (1868–1885), Boucher gently, but with a moue of distaste, compares the fashions of the time to that of furniture upholstery:

[W]e see the reappearance of *polonaises*, a reminiscence of Louis XVI style; the outer gown completely showed the underskirt and formed a longer or shorter train at the back, edged with pleated frills, ruchings or passmenteries [lace] depending on the time . . . Other models consisted of *tunics* draped at the sides and forming bustles behind. *Aprons*, which were also draped, and scarves were added to these already overloaded forms, which echoed the extravagances of furniture upholstery, evoking the conglomeration of fashionable drawing-rooms crammed with full-fringed curtains, buttoned chairs, bibelots and plants.[75]

This heavily ornamented style, usually lumped under the ignominious title of "Victorian," has been blamed on the desires of the bourgeoisie to replicate the wealth of their social superiors, but lacking the "refined taste" of their betters, they had instead "misread" its elegance. It has also been said that the early nineteenth century was awash in a series of revivals of past styles dating from the baroque, with few innovations to enhance or enliven these "dead" styles. Both theories perhaps have some elements of truth, but I think Boucher comes closer to a more complex and revelatory explanation in his admonition that this was an era of strict rules on sartorial matters, calculated by the time of day, the nature of the event, and the class of the society attending—"all subject to almost ritual prescriptions, from which one could not depart without appearing lacking in education."[76] What is missing in this explanation is the seeming lack of innovation, a lack of something new to move female fashion into a notion of a progressive phenomenon.

Yet it *was* changing, and constantly. Couture designers were introducing new designs for each season, which were picked up in successive seasons by dressmakers and the emerging ready-to-wear producers for the lower classes. Fashion, introduced as a concept in this period of nascent modernity, "stands, almost by definition, for the absolutely new—for permanent novelty and constant, insatiable change . . . fashion is revolutionary, detached from the continuous progression of history and the rather static concept of beauty."[77] Yet, as previously acknowledged, this creation of a continual *new* was also redolent with the past. What we have judged as static styles in this period are—seen from the distance of time—actually reiterations of past styles with subtle differences and small innovations, such as the culotte. A flourish of accessories, hats, and undergarments appears in this first stage, but the most telling new development was in the innovative devices and solutions that allowed women to create and follow new styles without the cost of buying a new gown—what is now nicknamed DIY: do-it-yourself. Trim became the most common device for altering an old gown to resemble the current fashion, leading to what Boucher disdained as "overloaded ornamentation": not everyone is able to design.

Boucher describes the transformation of women's fashions of the latter nineteenth century as a significant change in profile brought on by industrialization. Waistlines, which had been brought up to beneath the bustline in the early neoclassical period, dropped in the early 1820s to normal positions and became, through the use of technologically enhanced corsetry, more "pronounced"—that is, much smaller, less natural. The skirt became fuller, longer, and heavier than the diaphanous folds of the neoclassical gowns, now using heavy textiles and trim to form a broad base at the hemline. The basic lines of Victorian fashion were then set: the female wasp-like silhouette was essentially formed by two conical shapes: the broad bustline enhanced by the release at the bust of the corset, the use of Bertha collars and trims that framed the décolleté, the tiny waist formed by an increasingly tight corset, and the long full-structured skirt supported by various layers of crinolines.[78]

But from 1825 to about 1850, the female costume was influenced by the romantic movement and by

> a new generation who preferred dreams to hard cash . . . as if to counter-balance the materialism and mediocrity of an excessively bourgeois class. They enlivened fashion with fantasy that was often wanton, enchanted by the ephemeral. Leg-o-mutton sleeves accentuated the top "cone" of the profile, and added a romantic touch. Gowns had flounced skirts, and were trimmed with embroideries and ribbons, bonnets and muffs, in bright colors.[79]

Yet is the period from 1850 to 1868 marks the moment of radical change brought about by industrialization. From about 1852, the crinoline—after having disappeared for some time—now appears in an expanded form. Women's clothes became heavy and solemn. The closed bonnet, crinoline gowns, and tippets and shawls were elements of this style. The chief characteristics of this period were the great width at the base of the gown, giving the profile a pyramid shape, and a pronounced increase in lavishly embroidered and lace-trimmed undergarments.[80] In addition, in 1858, Charles Worth founded the first modern haute couture firm in Paris, changing forever the course of the feminine profile's shape from one created by female dressmakers to one dominated by male couturiers.

Yet to fully understand the profound difference in the clothing and fashions between the genders, we must first "undress" the Victorian woman to appreciate the layers of concealment and masquerade that composed the fashions of the time. Victorians developed a dual aspect to their culture: a proper bourgeois surface of morality with rigid family values stood in contrast to the gothic demimonde, eccentric social practices and obsessions, and a welter of landmark pornography: "A characteristic feature of the Victorian middle class was its peculiarly intense preoccupation with rigid boundaries . . . crisis and boundary confusion were warded off and contained by fetishes, absolution rituals and liminal scenes."[81] It is the specific liminal boundary that marks the visible outer clothing from the invisible underclothing wherein the vocabulary of fetish fashion emerges. To understand the role of fetish in fashion, we must transverse this boundary, for in the undergarments of the nineteenth-century female, and the neurotic associations and prohibitions associated with this culture in the midst of crisis, we will discover the founding forms of fetish fashion.

The obsessive concern over purity and cleanliness signified the nineteenth-century cultural crisis and intense abjection of the "contamination" that foreign colonial subjects and feminine bodies came to represent. The association of these individuals with bodily fluids and excrement spurred an intense and eccentric cultural fetishizing of these vestments, which provided not only protection for the body from outside contamination but also a way to constrain, manipulate, and label female bodies. The image of the Victorian bourgeois woman was fully "pictured" by the end of the eighteenth century: "the triumph of the useless woman was complete. Robbed of her productive labor, the middle-class woman became fitted . . . only for an ornamental place in society. There drooping prettily in the faded perfume of watercolors and light embroidery, she lived only to adorn the worldly ambition of her husband."[82]

This "picturing" entailed a theatrical performance of respectability and leisure ensuring the perception of male success. The costumes for this drama bristled with specific details. Women's clothes were heavily layered with undergarments, corsets and bustles, gloves, skirts, and a collection of small accessories. All were obsessively detailed: lined with laces, ruffles, and trim in accordance with a rigidly specific, though constantly changing, and heavily coded fashion. Undergarments were white or the natural muslin color as a boundary of cleanliness protecting against the moist contamination of the female body: the source of feminine fluids, especially menstrual blood. Foucault, in his work on the repressive regimes of the Victorian era, reminds us that "the body [became] a mode of specification of individuals,"[83] and the female individual thus created was, in its mythic bourgeois form, a youthful femininity of purity, pink-tinged delicacy, and virginal sexuality. For women and especially for little girls, the flurry of skirts and petticoats, flowers and ribbons became, then as now, a closeted culture of a fictional hyperfemininity and a space of imagined safety and delight-filled narcissism for the abject gender to create an abject community.[84]

Yet like most cultural artifacts from the Victorian period, this image of femininity is full of contradictions and ambiguities, hidden powers and subversive sexualities.

The artifacts of this feminine culture were structured through the eccentricities of the male gaze, under the over-rationalized and instrumental patriarchy of the time. Then as now, whether the designers were male or female, the effect and forms were dictated by popular images of the "ideal woman." The highly eroticized hourglass figure, made possible by the ingenious and complex construction of the corset, was likened at the time to bees or wasps, with the insect queen the very model of the hyper*maternal* female. Like Queen Victoria herself, who reveled and celebrated the role of the maternal as the ideal female, this image overemphasized a generous bust, a tiny waist, and a protuberant behind, accentuating and situating ideal femininity in the reproductive mode. Yet, in a subversive turn, women may have appropriated the corset not as a punitive restriction but as a source of individual desire. Art historian David Kunzle suggests, "[F]ar from being oppressed by their corsets, nineteenth century tight-lacers were sexually liberated female fetishists who found physical pleasure in the embrace of the corset."[85]

Beginning with the nineteenth-century female nude body, we add the first layer, underclothing, which can be separated broadly into two kinds. *Underlinens*—such as chemise, drawers, petticoat, corset covers, and combinations—protected the valuable corset, dress, and outer clothing from the body, whereas *structural underwear*, such as corsets, bustles, crinolines, and bust-improvers, created the fashionable silhouette. A chemise (a cotton or muslin sleeveless shirt-like garment) and a pair of drawers were worn next to the skin. The chemise protected the corset and dress from the moisture and soil on the skin, and because laundering occurred much less frequently than in contemporary times, this was an important consideration. By the 1860s, the chemise was usually made of cotton and often embroidered. During the 1870s, the dress bodice (called a cuirasse bodice) became very long and tight. The chemise became less voluminous, shorter, and often sleeveless. By the end of the century, the chemise had become a very simply cut, sleeveless garment with narrow shoulders and a round, square, V-, or heart-shaped neckline, very highly decorated with lace and embroidery and made of fine cotton or linen and even silk.[86]

The drawers were initially formed from two pieces of muslin that were linked by a drawstring, leaving the crotch open—a fact that might enlighten contemporary readers to the actual allure of the French cancan dancers of the nineteenth-century Moulin Rouge. Examples and patterns of drawers exist in the early part of the century, suggesting that although clearly some women wore them, perhaps some did not. These early forms extended to below the knee and joined together at the waistband. A surfeit of fabric at the waist and legs overlapped, providing some coverage and warmth. Many had

> drawstring casings at the waist and they generally all tied or buttoned at the centre back. During the 1860s and '70s, drawers were sometimes gathered into kneebands and often had a hip yoke to reduce fullness at the waist. The version with kneebands became known as knickerbockers (abbreviated to knickers) . . . With the onset of the cage crinoline in the 1850s, it became essential to wear drawers, for warmth and due to the risk of embarrassing accidents.[87]

The corset was put on over the chemise and drawers to shape the figure. The corset is, of course, one of the most controversial objects of the nineteenth century, alternately and vociferously vilified as a health hazard, as a narcissistic and pathetic tactic for a youthful body, and as a ridiculous feminine extravagance. With his usual gift of overstatement, Napoleon called the corset an "assassin of the human race . . . which maltreats their progeniture, presages frivolous taste and imminent decadence,"[88] linking corsets to abortion. Yet Kunzle also demonstrates that within the emerging new magazines for women (primarily edited by men) were frequent testimonies by women who loved the sensation and the appearance of "tightlacing." He cites 1863 as the first moment in which a letter written to a Victorian journal presented a favorable commentary on the corset: "[I]t is blatantly, unapologetically, exhibitionistic" in its praise for the "harmless mode of giving a graceful slenderness to the figure."[89]

Corsets of various form and use have been around since the ancient Greeks, dying out only to reappear over and again. In the late 1860s, a craze for tight-lacing emerged when the skirt became gored and slim-fitting at the waist. New industrial technologies, textiles, and processes had developed in corset manufacture and brought on a storm of corset designs that created nearly constant swiveling in preferences for the profile of the female torso, as fashion accelerated under the new conditions of consumerism. During the 1870s and 1880s, spoon busks were also used, which consisted of curved front clasps that widened over the stomach. The corset had been worn under the petticoat until the cuirasse dress of the 1870s innovated the practice of fashionable women wearing the under-petticoat beneath the corset. The corset tended to elevate and accentuate the bust, flatten the rounded stomach, and nip in the waist, leading to variations of the maternal hourglass figure. By the 1890s, bust, waist, and hips became smoothed with a straight-fronted corset that pushed the bust out in a continuous whole (the mono-bosom) and tilted the wearer forward, heralding the *S*-shaped stance of the Edwardian era.[90]

After the corset, an under-petticoat was worn over all of these pieces, sometimes as an entire all-in-one garment with a petticoat bodice, or sometimes as a waist petticoat with a separate corset cover—a "separate petticoat bodice which was either waist length or longer, front-opening and fitted to the figure by means of front darts and sometimes curved side back seams. The cut reflected fashion and could be sleeveless, short- or long-sleeved."[91] The corset cover provided the dress with one more layer of sanitary consideration; it also provided a "modesty panel" for the delicate décolleté revealed in diaphanous summer and evening dresses. The separate corset covers of the late 1880s and 1890s were usually called camisoles, early versions of the present-day camisole.

A structural skirt "support" such as a crinoline or a bustle could be worn over these, depending on the prevailing fashion, which greatly vacillated over the latter half of the century. This was then covered by at least two decorative petticoats that sometimes became the underskirt of the dress itself. The alluring petticoat has always had a dual role as an undergarment and a structural garment. It provided warmth and modesty and, by alternately masking and creating "peek-a-boo" revelations of the contours of the legs, created the nineteenth-century fetish of the "well-turned ankle." It also helped to shape the dress and therefore mirrored the cut of the skirt. Horizontal drawstrings at various positions allowed adjustment of the petticoat (cut from straight lengths of fabric), below which it might expand into ruffles or a flounced train that could be detached.[92]

It was fashionable to wear many petticoats prior to the invention of the cage crinoline, which appeared in Paris in 1855. A true object of the Industrial Revolution, the cage crinoline was made from riveted circles of steel, concentric and graduated in diameter to sometimes enormous dimensions, and they were suspended by cloth supports from the waistband. Later, the lighter watchspring steel would be used to support the ever-widening skirts. After 1866, skirts and crinolines gradually began to shrink in diameter, but they began to enlarge behind, enhancing the buttocks, to form the bustle. In 1867, at the highlight of the maternal profile made fashionable by Queen Victoria, the crinoline was greatly reduced and a new emphasis began to be placed on the rear of the dress, throwing the fashionable female profile into an extreme distortion. Bustles were either large, down-filled pads or frills of stiff fabric that tied around the waist. They were often called "dress-improvers" because they threw the skirt out in a dome at the back, thus "improving" its wasp-like silhouette. Bustles were to be worn with or without the shrunken crinoline. The bustle quickly declined by the mid-1870s and virtually disappeared by 1889. From the 1890s, the fashionable silhouette would apparently depend entirely upon the wearer's corseted figure and be augmented discreetly by small bustle pads tied around the waist or a flourish of ribbons and bows.[93] Finally, the visible layers of the dress, shoes, stockings, fans, gloves, hats, veils, jewelry, umbrellas, and purses could be put on over this heavily layered invisible assemblage of underwear.

According to Stephen Kern, "In no other age throughout history was the human body, in particular the female body, so concealed and disfigured by clothing." Whereas men's "drab" and "static" clothing merely hid the body, women's clothing constituted an attack on the body as much as an effort to conceal it—amounting to a kind of "mummification."[94] That is to say, women were so surrounded and saturated not only with the extreme layers of clothing but also with the signifiers of nineteenth-century femininity: the ribbons, ruffles, and bows as well as the misogyny, prejudice, and condescension. These various layers created a shape and profile of the feminine that was distorted and coerced into the hourglass figure, the wasp, the reproductive machine that denoted the "proper" feminine person. What a woman *was* had to do with her social rank and class—construed through marriage or patrimony—and, with that, the consequent presumed content of her character. According to Steele, women wore these uncomfortable physically restrictive clothes because they were "caught between the contradictory demands to be both physically desirable and morally proper."[95] What about this profile was "physically desirable"? The body was perceived as "bad"—that is, associated with the sensual, the sexual—and so it was hidden, disfigured, and mutilated. In common with most Victorian dress reformers, feminist fashion historians today tend to perceive nineteenth-century men's clothing as vastly superior to women's costumes of the same era and interpret progress in large part in terms of the supposed approach of women's clothes to the "utilitarian" masculine model. Steele asks "whether there is anything intrinsically superior about dark colors, unerotic tailoring, and an absence of ornamentation."[96]

Although women were rigidly classified as either "Madonnas or Magdalens, both wives and whores wore clothing that was simultaneously concealing and indecent."[97] The notion that "respectable sexual ideology = a highly restrictive sexual morality" was functionally integrated into the social and economic structure of society: "Victorian sexual mores were essentially bourgeois, associated with the capitalist economy, and centered on the ideal of sexual continence (saving) except for the purposes of procreation (spending)."[98] Despite problems of logic and the lack of evidence, the theory of respectable sexual ideology has strongly influenced current interpretations of Victorian fashions.

Between Iterations

This is not to say that there were no developments in the fetish fashions and performances in the early part of the twentieth century. In fact, these had been flourishing in various underground magazines and publications throughout the twentieth century and in very private clubs. In the United States, the chronology of fetish development occurred in three distinct phases that bring their particular foci to bear on the later postmodern flourishing.

The *European Fetish* (c. 1928),[99] apparently primarily heterosexual in orientation, was based in representations of industrial materials such as leather, rubber, and (in the latter postwar period of the 1960s) metal and PVC; these were fashioned into "bizarre" costumes, uniforms, and shoes and boots. They appeared in various underground but widely distributed magazines. By the 1930s, the key fetishist magazine in the world was *London Life*. Available literally around the globe, it was a worldwide advertising venue for craftspeople who created fetishistic clothing as well as for sellers of erotic books.[100] The *American Fetish* style, particularly in the 1930s and early 1940s, was highly influenced by the European style, similar in both the forms of media used and in the fashions that emerged: "During the 1930–1960 period key innovators of the American Fetish style were located in New York City, with imitators in a number of other locations, particularly California."[101] And by the late 1940s, a number of distinctive products for a largely heterosexual audience, including magazines and photography, appeared: "[K]ey themes included bizarre practices and fetishistic costume, bondage, transvestism, and female domination."[102] And finally, *Gay Leather*—the third phase—became prominent in the mid-twentieth century and was predominantly an S/M style that developed out of the gay leather subculture in the United States. Beinvenu states that this subculture evolved from the postwar motorcycle clubs and bars that appeared particularly in California and in large cities such as Los Angeles, New York, and Chicago during the 1950s and 1960s. The Gay Leather style injected a "hyper-masculine, 'butch' aesthetic that is self-consciously the antithesis of effeminate gay stereotypes"[103] and brought the heavy connotations of masculinity, violence, and aggressive sexuality of black leather into contemporary fetish forms.

The Second Great Iteration: The Postmodern Era (1968–Present)

> In Walter Benjamin's interpretation of the modern age as a vision of hell, fashion was placed in the prime role as the signifier of the ceaseless repetitiveness that he saw as its chief characteristic.
>
> Rebecca Arnold, *Fashion, Desire and Anxiety: Image and Morality in the 20th Century*[104]

The Postwar Period (1950–1980)

In my own memory, it was the 1975 shocking outing of transgendered Dr. Richard Raskind, male naval officer and amateur tennis player, as Renee Richards, female, that sounded the alert to the gender panic brewing in the nascent postmodern era. However, in conversation with other scholars,[105] I was reminded of different eruptions of transgressive gender and sexual revelations among the assassinations and colonial wars that occurred in rapid succession during the latter half of the twentieth century, marking in repetitive blows the changes that exponentially increased the volatility of society. The rupture that was to sink the albatross, to yank modernist society out of its sleepy postwar confidence, was the abrupt rising of the radical divergence known and felt by all as the "paradigm shift," later called the "postmodern turn." The Stonewall riots of 1969, a "routine police raid on the Stonewall Inn, a Christopher Street hangout for gays, run by the Mafia, prompted not cowed obedience from the customers but uncharacteristic fury and outrage."[106] This was followed by the vituperative railings by a paranoid and conservative society through the likes of Anita Bryant, and the riots were rarely spoken of in public without disgust, denigration, and a nervous snigger. The proud demand for acceptance of male homosexuals came as a terrifying shock to a culturally middle-class society for whom the word *homosexual* had been reserved for the hushed tones of scandal and shame. Further unsettling was the nationally televised shredding of the Loud family in the first "reality" PBS television series (1971–1973), in which a horrified public watched as Lance Loud, the eldest son, confessed to the entire country that he was a homosexual. And later, the "typical parents," Bill and Pat Loud, broke up and divorced in front of a stunned American public.

It was becoming difficult to believe in the peculiar American illusion of the universality of the "normal," of an idealized, codified, and recognizable middle-class heterosexual family unit. This particular illusion featured domesticated females in figure-defining clothes (referred to at the time as the "New Sweetheart Line"[107]) and positioned them in terms of their sexual availability, while the men of business continued to wear the modernist asexual uniform of the dark suit. Just as in the late nineteenth century, by the late twentieth century, intense changes in the fundamental levels of society called for "the collapse of the 'grand narratives' . . . and their replacement with the 'little narratives' in the wake of technologies which . . . transformed our notion of what constitutes knowledge."[108] There was not one aspect of life at the time that was not radically altered by the changes brought about the destruction of those "grand narratives." This highly visualized conception of middle-class America had been inculcated into the postwar culture to the point of a complacent naturalization, but it was then fragmented in the space of a decade essentially by the rapid advances of technologies. These innovations took us all to the moon and allowed us advanced communication devices, quicker travel in cars exchanged for new ones every year, to live longer and die less often, to eat foreign foods, and to wear fashionable but inexpensive clothes made abroad. But it also led us to experience the massive influence of a deeply invasive and dramatically mediated advertisement establishment, which commodified virtually every aspect of life through a subversive and powerful corporate/military/industrial complex that had colonized the globe.

The civil rights movement in America had spawned the Stonewall riots and went on to reawaken the feminist movement and an array of other "identity" political movements, throwing the political balance into an extremely liberal cast. After the shocking revolt in Paris in May 1968, "massive confrontations between police and students brought workers out on a general strike and brought the government to the point of collapse . . . followed by clashes between police and students in countries all around the world, [which] would have a lasting political impact."[109] Not only were world politics altered, but a newly emerging, Marxist-based analytic method of conceptualizing social relations through objects, referred to as critical theory, began to influence all areas of academic work. This umbrella term had sundered into a variety of approaches of textual criticism, including both structuralism and poststructuralism, postmodernism, and psychoanalytic and semiotic analyses. These works developed into, among many others, the concepts of Derridean deconstruction, systems of difference, and "conceptual orderings (such as those of 'objectivity' and 'subjectivity', 'self' and 'other')."[110]

Expanded Identity Movements

By the late 1960s, the women's movement had intersected with critical theory and had begun to develop work that questioned the very foundations of societal notions of sex and gender, which had been so carefully constructed in the late nineteenth century. Up to this point, the notions of sex and gender had been, in most mainstream cases, conjoined and conflated to refer to the genitalia of the two established gender choices: male or female. This "reduction to gender as sex (which would be to see gender differences as themselves biologically determined) may be understood as a key move in the ideological justification of patriarchy."[111] One of the first moves in critical theory was to unlink these two terms and establish sex as biologically determined, but with the additional trouble of the intrasexual—long a secret sexual determination that was historically considered a birth defect and was then hurriedly assigned to one or the other sex by surgical intervention. Gender became a designation that was essentially a cultural education according to prescribed gender roles under what was now acknowledged as the modernist patriarchy.

Once gender and gender roles came under scrutiny, a welter of work from feminist critics—popularly termed third-wave feminists—appeared through their study of the marginalized feminine subject. There also emerged criticism on the other marginalized and therefore feminized subjects: cross-dressers, homosexuals, fetishists, drag queens, drag kings, and dominatrices and their fetishist family. Critics such as Elaine Showalter emerged. Showalter blazed the trail with her three phases of gender in literary theory. The first phase, *feminist critique,* comprised the earliest moments of examining literature for the underlying ideologies of the patriarchy. The last phase was termed *gender theory,* in which theory is generated from research into ideological constructions and their interpellation of feminine subjects by male and female authors. But it is primarily the psychoanalytical feminist theories developed by Luce Irigaray, Julia Kristeva, Hélène Cixous, and Judith Butler that actually began to critique the primacy of male heterosexuality in culture and consequently troubled Freud's and Marx's still-standing theories of the fetish. Initially, the problem was Freud's assertion that the fetish was—as a uniquely male affliction—a response to male horror at discovering that his mother did not have a penis and that his powerful father has castrated her and may castrate him for his patricidal oedipal fantasies:

> In normal development . . . this castration threat prompts the boy to turn away from the "castrated" mother and to identify with the father, taking up a heterosexual subject position in the process. The fetishist instead disavows sexual difference through a fetish that is a substitute for the mother's imaginary phallus . . . the fetish serves to repair the imagined mutilations of the mother; it masks lack, and protects the fetishist from his fears of castration. By mitigating castration anxiety, the fetish can make sexual relations possible.[112]

In responding to the profoundly subordinate position where this, and all patriarchal theoretical and cultural constructions, had placed the female subject, many feminist critics such as Judith Butler have suggested that "the category of 'gender' as a human construct [was] enacted by a vast repetition of social performance."[113] The differences in biological, psychological, and cultural experiences of males and females—the existing sexual categories—eventually came into question as products of a patriarchal male heterosexual culture. Gender theory became a major topic not only among academics, critics, and cultural theorists but also in the mainstream press. Initially much of its theoretical rigor came through the work of this same group of feminist theorists. Summarized briefly, they proposed,

> In Western culture, the imaginary body which dominates on a cultural level is a male body . . . [and this cultural condition thus suggests] that Western culture privileges identity, unity, and sight—all of which [are suggested to be] associated with male anatomy . . . that fields such as philosophy, psychoanalysis, science and medicine are controlled by this imaginary . . . since Freud was unable to imagine another perspective, his reduction of women to male experience resulted in viewing women as defective men.[114]

Once the door opened to marginal subjects, a category now referred to as queer theory emerged; although the name suggests—and in fact includes—a discourse of gay and lesbian subjects, it actually describes a larger, more inclusive discourse of diverse sexualities and identities. By its postmodern inclusion of a plethora of identities and sexualities performed and lived at all levels of society, queer theory embraces virtually all non-normative categories of identities and sexualities outside the gates of what Judith Butler described as the "heterosexual matrix" or, as she later referred to it, a "heterosexual hegemony."[115] Subjects within this highly surveilled boundary are confined to the meanings of a rigidly male-centered heterosexual and patriarchal ideology. Outside this boundary are all other genders, sexualities, and identities. Queer theory began the process of outing, marking, and identifying subjects whose ontological aspects, in some cases, defied categorical descriptions.

As these subjects were revealed to exist in every area of human occupation, the walls of the matrix began to crumble, and thus began in the 1980s a parade of transgressive performances, literatures, art, music, and personalities that, despite the culture's conservative political nature, were given high exposure in the entertainment world of the press, television, film, and (by the end of the decade) the Internet. Individuals and groups such as Boy George, Madonna, Joan Jett, Queen, David Bowie, Jeff Koons, Leigh Bowery, Andres Serrano, and many others all transgressed the boundaries of the heterosexual matrix and yet commanded enormous attention with their work in the theoretical discourse of critical studies. A 1992 book by Madonna, *Sex*—which still appeared in 2010 "BookFinders' *100 Most Sought After Out-of-Print Books List*"[116]—showcased photographs of Madonna and friends engaged in a graphic array of fetish practices in a straightforward and fashion-forward style. Madonna outed the fashions of the heretofore profoundly covert world of fetish performance and fashions, which had since the late nineteenth century created a solid collection of distinctly fetish objects based on the underwear of nineteenth-century women. This situation mirrored fashion's radically expanding consumption and visibility, revealing a "process by which fashion has come to play so crucial a role in conjuring with and renegotiating of the power relations of status and identity."[117]

Postmodern Sumptuary Panic

In the nineteenth century, the dandy embodied his singular profile of masculinity—as a defense against the encroaching powers of the Others: the "new woman," the Chérette, and the homosexual male, who threatened the vulnerable male hegemony—and created a *habit noir* uniform that foreclosed and veiled any dangerous slippages into the Others' identities. In the contemporary American culture of the early twenty-first century, the "bro-ski"[118] has assumed the postmodern veil of masculinity, adopting the boyish uniform of oversize, baggy but cropped cargo pants, polo or T-shirt, backward ball cap, and tennis shoes worn by all ages of men to armor themselves against the same threat of slippage into the Other, in addition to using organized codes that reference this ubiquitous eternally adolescent uniform. The paradox of this imago or "ideal state" that both these masculine fashions represent was marked in the mid-twentieth century with the much-discussed concern of the "mass man": the modernist cultural edict glorified the "heroic" individual male achiever, but still demanded that men "fit in." Now in postmodernity, men were losing their automatic authoritarian sheen to the Others, who were proliferating and extending bodily frontiers, which brought our "mass man" new fears of not fitting in. As Fernbach acknowledges,

> Faced with the postmodern cry that the body is under erasure as the boundaries of the body are being exploded in the quest to arrive at the post-human, it is not surprising that contemporary fears of body dissolution and fragmentation arise. It is likely that in the postmodern condition pre-oedipal anxieties about fragmentation and dissolution, along with the correlative desire to merge with the greater whole will be heightened, especially for the male subject, whose sense of wholeness and experience of being "at the center of things" is rapidly collapsing.[119]

Women's clothing had begun in the late nineteenth century to access and emulate male styles—particularly of the dandy. Throughout the twentieth century, the adapted men's styles had become progressively more identical to the actual clothing of males. By the end of World War II, young women had adopted the uniform—and even the actual clothing—of the returning young men from war, whose rebellion against the expectations of the older generation had resulted in new forms of music and culture. Young women wore the denim jeans, the oversized shirts, and penny loafer shoes of men for casual dress. Yet no one cared; it was not considered at all transgressive or subversive, but instead, it was "cute" to see the newly termed *teen-aged* girl in her cross-dressed uniform.

By the end of the twentieth century and continuing on into the twenty-first, women who had gained position in high offices, and especially in politics, were noted for wearing unflattering suits based on the male model in dull colors, termed *power suits*. Despite the attempt at a uniform for women in power, they were an adaptation—though not a particularly skilled one—of the male *habit noir*, after a century still the uniform of men in power. Instead, women even then seemed to understand the male body to represent all cultural images of power, identity, beauty, unity, and sight—concepts that continued to be associated with male anatomy—and further, woman was still simply a "defective man." Women in power continued to be coded as "masculine" because of the durability of the image of the modern male as the fetishized authoritarian subject. The feminine could not be "pictured" as being in power: no models except the maternal model had any power, and her power was one of the castrated male. Yet there was one profoundly underground exception: the dominatrix of the fetish culture.

1960s–1970s: Mods and Rockers

[T]he opening up of popular culture in the 1960s sexualized all areas of design and its representation. Eroticism became a playful way of flaunting new moral codes that mocked the hypocrisy of the establishment.

Rebecca Arnold, *Fashion, Desire and Anxiety*[120]

In the fiery cultural cauldron of violence and change that was the 1960s, a fashion revolution for both males and females emerged in the United Kingdom: "[T]he Mods and The Rockers were two groups that were closely related . . . Each group represented opposite tastes with regard to a number of social conventions such as clothing, grooming, [and] music."[121] The revolution began in the late 1950s in Scotland Road in Liverpool, a local hotspot for pubs and young people from the working-class and immigrant families. One of the groups that emerged were the Mods, teens who tended to dress in upper-middle-class formal dress and understood themselves to be "modern" (hence the name Mods) and stylish: "[T]he Mod boys dressed in suits, neat narrow trousers, and pointed shoes. The girls displayed a boyish image. They darkened their eyes and wore their hair short to fit a unisex type of culture."[122] They expanded their territory to London and South East England and were followers of the latest fashions; as the 1960s continued, they were frequently the innovators of fashion. Part of the their "gear" was the motor scooter, "a Lambretta GT 200 or a Vespa GS 160," and they were associated with jazz, rhythm and blues, the Rolling Stones, the Yardbirds, the Pretty Things, the Kinks, the Cyril Davis All-Stars, the Downliners, and the Small Faces.[123] Their culture was exemplified by the Who:

The most popular and revolutionary band who could be labeled as Mods themselves were the High Numbers, later renamed The Who. They wore Mod outfits, had Mod hairstyles, and sang blues-based songs about being Mods, such as "I'm the Face," and "My Generation." The Who's performance often included Pete Townshend (guitarist) smashing his guitar into the speakers, as well as Keith Moon (drummer) knocking over his drums. The Who's violence on stage personified the aggression inherent in the Mod subculture.[124]

The Rockers also began in Liverpool's Scotland Road and were in many respects the antithesis of the Mods. The Rockers get their name from their obsession with rock-and-roll music and their emulation of the black-leathered Hell's Angels: "[T]heir style consisted of jeans, boots and leather jackets . . . They wore black leather and studs, had anti-authority beliefs, and projected an easy rider nomadic romanticism. The Rockers lived for the present, with a scruffy, masculine, 'bad boy' image."[125] Their hair was shaggy, they rode motorcycles—either a Triumph or a Norton—and hung out in greasy spoon diners and restaurants. John Lennon of the Beatles was photographed dressed in Rocker gear in his early days. Newly emerging fashion designs in the 1960s reflected elements of both groups in the so-called Carnaby Street fashions, the location of the independent young fashion designers who were associated with the youth subcultures of the time.

Both groups, and the succeeding groups and subgroups of the burgeoning "youth culture" of the 1960s and 1970s, attacked the sexual mores of the "straight" culture of the adult establishment. In addition to constant riots over the Vietnam War, the civil rights of various marginalized cultures, and the emerging environmental movement was the sexual revolution of "free love." Although free love initially centered on heterosexual love, the Stonewall riots "outed" homosexuality, and it was embraced as a particularly radical position within the movement. Though true acceptance was slow to emerge, nevertheless the gay rights movement opened the door for a series of homosexual, bisexual, and eventually fetishist performers such as Leigh Bowery, Boy George, Madonna, Andy Warhol, David Bowie, and others in the 1980s.

But fetish remained still very much underground as yet, despite the groundbreaking fashion designs of Vivienne Westwood and Malcolm McLaren in the 1970s. An exception was found in the fashion photography of Guy Bourdin and Helmut Newton:

> During the 1970s the pages of French Vogue became an erotic interplay between [Bourdin's] hyperreal colour images and the starker, more blatantly fetishistic styling of Helmut Newton's work. Both benefited from the immediacy of the image, which commanded an instant non-intellectual emotional response, an instant desire for the fantasy they provided, and yet an equally powerful sense of uncertainty in the face of such explicit artificiality.[126]

In both black-and-white and color, these were new sorts of fashion images—dark, erotic, drugged-looking, with an undercurrent of violence and death. Young women were posed as powerful, sometimes sinister, sometimes vanquished femme fatales. Arnold suggests, "Glazed models became twilight vamps, and long-held fears concerning the sanity of women who gave themselves up to sensuality and eroticism were brought to the surface of glossy photographs."[127] This sort of fetish-infused photography only increased in visibility during the latter part of the twentieth century, and it continued to do so in the early twenty-first century as fetish began to emerge in fashion itself.

Vivienne Westwood and the Introduction of Punk and Fetish Fashions

> Westwood's approach to design as a means to assert a personal political stance used this anxiety, exposing hidden desires, with pornographic imagery and slogans.
>
> Rebecca Arnold, *Fashion, Desire and Anxiety*[128]

Vivienne Westwood and her punk-rock partner, Malcolm McLaren (of the band Sex Pistols), awoke the sleeping potential of the fetish aesthetic with a kiss: they opened a shop in London called Sex in 1970 that was "perhaps the most influential forerunner of fetish haute couture."[129] Her style was "associated with transgressing social codes" and challenging "orthodox notions about gender, sexuality and the body."[130] Using a punk-informed pastiche of historical forms and fetish identities, Westwood employed gender constructions as styles rather than cultural roles, as images rather than edicts, breaking up the modernist linkages of class, culture, and gender into a panoply of fantasy identities pasted together with wit and humor and a not-so-hidden political agenda. Her appropriation of fetish forms (the corset, bondage straps, black leather jackets) and the predominance of black in her fashions all signified fetish obsessions and all the sexual and erotic implications they represent. She introduced designs using vintage-style petticoats, screen-printed T-shirts with quotes such as the Sex Pistol's "No Future" juxtaposed with imitations of Tom of Finland's gay guys, and pieces of underwear collaged together to form collections that flew in the face of mainstream couture design. Overtly sexual, provocative, and erotic, her designs glorified the working-class clothing of the emerging punk bands rather than the upper-class, sophisticated couture of the mainstream studios.

She introduced the notion of androgyny with mixed indications of gender and the practice of S/M with her safety-pin ornamentation. Androgyny opens up and disseminates gender as ornament or aesthetic; consequently, it tends to oscillate between cues and proposes instead a third gender, an amalgam of gender indications. This was the landscape of the punk scene, with its revolutionary fashion, music, and culture, its emerging vintage and DIY processes, its historical conglomerations and rich sights, and its most important feat, the opening of gender roles and sexual liberation. As Arnold notes, "Vivienne Westwood's punk styles of the 1970s [signaled] the breakup of fashion's smooth surface . . . and did not just signify a contemptuous disrespect for social hypocrisy; it also reflected the sense of discontent of a generation, which wanted clothing to provide a costume for their angry lives, not an unreal fantasy of pleasure."[131] One way she accomplished this was to incorporate into her clothing such radically transgressive images and signs as the Nazi swastika, elongated nude penises, bare breasts, and the Queen with a safety pin through her nose. These were elements of societal fetishes that acted as naturalized signs of things such as patriotism (the Queen) or, alternatively, abject signs either considered perverse (nude penises) or representing heinous beliefs (Nazi swastikas). But Westwood removed them from their accepted contexts to reposition them all on the level of aesthetic sign, allowing their patinas of emotional or moral excess to be outlined, caricatured, and parodied. The result was that "Punk created another world, parallel to the 'norm' . . . where skinny youths flaunted the violent secrets of sado-masochism in bondage suits and unraveling string jumpers, and swaggered with cocky delight at the outrage they inevitably provoked."[132]

Yet what most provoked the critics of the time was the way in which she abrogated the female imago in her submissive position as pretty little sex object and legitimated the dangerous, hostile, and erotic woman of power. Westwood scoffed at the thin young body as ideal and later, in her sixties, had a nude photograph taken of herself that suggested another option for feminine beauty. This radical shift in the notion of the feminine ideal was the first real movement in fashion away from an ideal that had placed women in the second-class seat for centuries, and although the earlier ideal was still not entirely dispensed with, the culture rocked with the radical potential emerging in the fashion history.

1980s: The New Romanticism

What the punk scene and Westwood's fashions thus indicated was the shocking insight that "masculinity was as much a masquerade as femininity."[133] This was indeed a dangerous thought: much of the world had rested contentedly in the sureness of male superiority and authority for most of its history. The revelations of postmodernity knocked the legs out from under the patriarchal culture, rendering it unstable and initiating a reckless lurching from fundamentalist conservatism to radical liberalism and back again that has lasted into the twenty-first century. One of the umbrella terms for this period in fashion is "The New Romanticism." It began as many fashions began in this period—with a new pop music style:

> The New Romantics were a music genre in the 1980s generally considered to be a sub genre of the New Wave movement . . . There has been debate about whether the New Romantics were a new musical genre in their own right or whether they were merely a natural progression of the punk era . . . In the punk corner people say that the New Romantics were simply the natural progression that took place as punk became glamorized . . . In the New Romantic corner they claim that the movement was born out of a working class background that was highly influenced by television. Being brought up on television as opposed to radio led to bands wanting to be the whole package[,] looks as well as sound.[134]

Because many of these early bands performed at the club The Blitz, they came to be known as "The Blitz Kids." What made them different from the punksters was their love of an excessive and rococo sense of glamour. It is a glamour conceived of by working-class young adults whose access to traditional notions of glamour was limited to television and Hollywood movie conceptions. Also, because of their economic position, they tended to make their costumes and do their own makeup. As a result, their style was heavy in rich details cobbled together in a pastiche of different historic styles—though most frequently from the seventeenth-century rococo—and effects, including heavily and dramatically applied makeup. The characters they created were bizarre and even at times clown-like; in that they presented gender as a mere aesthetic effect, they "theatricalized cross-dressing for both men and women."[135] To use a term supposedly created in the 1960s, costumes were frequently "uni-sex";[136] that is, they presented either various aspects of both genders or no gender, to the extent that *unisex* became a singular nondiscriminating designation that merges gender and sexual difference into a positive unified conception, that negates any specific gender indication, and that is acceptable to both. However, despite the high-minded definition and its gestures toward equality, "uni-sex dress has always been essentially masculine in style."[137]

But it is the term *romantics* that signifies the rupture from modernity. It was precisely the romanticism of the late eighteenth and nineteenth centuries that modernism had revolted against. Romanticism rejected rationalism with its celebration of fantasy, strong emotion, aesthetics, and the exotic. Romantic works of art and poetry presented rich sights of untamed nature, romantic love, and folktales with a wealth of colorful detail and fantastic effect. Modernism sought to rationalize, industrialize, de-historicize, and de-fetishize—or so thought its practitioners—the design of objects. In the rupture that occurred between modernism and postmodernism in the 1980s, the reins of culture, held in the modernist period by men of power, were increasingly wrenched away by a pluralistic, youthful, and underground culture that reversed the trends of modernism with the riotous return of the popular culture's emotional, exotic, and DIY historical fashions. Though even in the contemporary period these movements are relegated to the category of a subculture, nevertheless, these and the succeeding movements toward the spectacular, the pastiche of historical forms, and the revolution in gender and sexual significations have utterly transformed the mainstream culture: "By exposing masculinity as artifice, the lie that masculinity as natural and fixed collapsed."[138]

1990s: Artifice, Pastiche, and Spectacle

Despite the fact that fashion is an arena dedicated to novelty, indeed could be said to fetishize novelty, in the work of such designers the present was constantly invaded by images of the past that seeped in, settled into the cracks and colonized the terrain of "the new."

Caroline Evans[139]

By the 1990s, the tenets of modernism had back-flipped to the opposing pole, and postmodernism had become the cultural catwalk wherein fashion strutted an array of highly eroticized and fetish-influenced fashions in extravagantly produced shows. Evans notes, "[T]he work of a range of designers at the end of the century . . . suggested the body as a site simultaneously of perfection and decay, drawing attention to the fascination of beauty and horror entwined."[140] Many who had been part of the modernist culture decried decadence, decay, and disorder as the death throes of its cultural standards and utopian goals: "[Frederick] Jameson argued that history was being plundered in contemporary visual culture to make a post-modern carnival, and that the incessant return to the past was itself a kind of deathly recycling of history which emptied it of meaning, rendering it bankrupt, good only for costume drama and fantasy."[141] But rather than a "recycling of history," it was in fact a manifestation of a rupture of massive change, as the powerful modernist culture crashed into a paradigm with a wrenching new technology—the Internet. The Internet provided an immovable force with which radically different modes of communication and representation eliminated any possibility of a return to the status quo. Modernism, with its male-cast eyes always on "the new," had not wanted to look at death, which was associated with the historical, the feminine, the dark, the moist, the closet, and the occult—the realm of the fetishist.

But in the 1990s, as couture began to reemerge as the origin of the latest fashion, designers threw open the doors of the closet and paraded its abject inhabitants down the catwalk in elaborate shows—reminiscent of Busby Berkeley films—using pent-up creativity and perhaps a bit of repressed vituperative energy. In spectacles of pastiche from never-existing eras, designs were redolent with colonial fusions,[142] fantasy films, noir, native and folk designs, and other quotations from the popular cultures of various eras and nations: all were merged into what became a drag performance of history and culture. Yet uniting all fashions from this time was the incessant citation of fetish forms that, although presented in innovative and gothic colorations, still carried many of the traditional indications from nineteenth-century costumes as their basis. The dark corsets, masks, high-heeled shoes and boots, gloves, and accessories of the dominatrix appeared in remarkable variations and emulations. Though Vivienne Westwood initially introduced the style, now designers across the board were using the fetish forms in all manner of fashion categories, even sportswear.

It was also a time of high consumption: a celebration of "bling," of the shiny commodity both as fashion and as fetish, which denoted wealth and a new emphasis on brand snobbery. Though fashions used the fetish forms, they oddly tended to eschew the erotic charge in favor of the shock charge, for a performance not about orgasmic pleasure but a horror-film type of excessive pleasure. Evans cites a Christian Dior catwalk show in which the program began as an imaginary letter from Freud to Jung:

> It read: "recently I glimpsed an explanation for the case of fetishism. So far it only concerns clothes, but it is probably universal." In the tongue-in-cheek parody . . .

[designer John] Galliano disguised the way in which the lost memory of commodity fetishism, rather than sexual fetishism, was evoked in the spectacular catwalk shows of the
1990s . . . [in which] commodity fetishism masqueraded as sexual fetishism. The reference to clothing fetishism was played out on the Dior catwalk as sexual "perversion," a
fiction that masked the real form of fetishism . . . that of commodity.[143]

It was indeed a time of ostentatious details: shiny brass, metallized leather finishes,
rococo gowns of brocades, satins, and colored petticoats juxtaposed with trainers,
heavy boots, ragged T-shirts, and metal corsets. It was a collision of values and meanings manifested in a mash-up of extremes from the clothing closets of culture. The orgasmic squeal came from the ecstasy of the commodity as easily as it came from the
sexual encounter, both phenomena projected as fetishistic in a screen-based culture.

2000 and Beyond: Lolita, Steampunk, and Other Historical and Fan Costume Movements

In addition to the couture innovations of the previous decade, new independent, fan-
based, and DIY clothing and costume movements emerged in the new millennium
and rapidly began to gain global recognition and emulation; these were based on
the fetishizing of various—although not necessarily related—cultural aspects such
as Victoriana; Japanese anime and manga; literary, television, and film narratives;
and vintage and consignment finds. Fetish as a specifically S/M practice, which was
outed by Madonna in the 1980s, now romped throughout the culture in its most pro-
fuse flowering of fetishizing practices. No longer confined to just sexual meanings,
fetish became manifest in the varied obsessions for the material detritus of objects
that cluttered not only the history of previous centuries but also the fictional histories
of popular cultures. Beginning with war reenactors and science fiction conventions
in the latter twentieth century, the obsession with masquerading as an Other (as a
fictional character in another time and place) in this period goes beyond the *lunatic
fringe*, so-called for their subversive and clandestine practices of enacting fantasy in
costumes. This phenomenon in the early part of the twenty-first century expanded
to the widespread and mainstreamed adaptation of masquerade, especially by young
people of all classes, genders, and interests. And by the end of the century's first
decade, even the affluent socialites noted in the *New York Times* were regularly seen
at masquerading events.

During this time, multiple categories of fetish fashion proliferated. Many, paradoxically, were associated with nineteenth-century fashions. Even the abject female
of the nineteenth century is reprised in her ornamental rococo mode, but with a de-
cided difference. The "Lolita," a Japanese street fashion that evolved in the same
early-postmodern period, was inspired by the clothing and general aesthetics of the
rococo and Victorian periods as represented in Japanese manga and anime. Both

young and increasingly older women adopted the "Lolita" style; some were cosplay-ers who fetishize anime and manga characters, whereas others fetishized the roman-ticized fiction of the life of little girls from the nineteenth century. As in the S/M version, it is not the actual subjects that are of interest as much as the mythic notion of Victorian girlhood: the same girlhood that has been the stuff of books for girls throughout the twentieth century. This global obsession is in some sense in reaction to the Western "business bitch" with her power suit and her masculine model. The Lolita is an ultrafeminine form that perhaps suggests a retrogressive attempt to se-cure gender forms against contemporary instability, but it also represents a compel-ling attempt to reinscribe the feminine form in fashion.

Steampunk, also an obsession with European Victoriana, addresses both the male and female fashions of the nineteenth century but "punked," that is, using the tac-tics of the punk era including DIY, a collision of fictional and pastiched authentic forms, "editorial" details, humor, and sexual innuendo. A fetish that has many more male adherents than usual, steampunk also includes "inventing" fictional Victorian machines and apparatuses, which are sometimes worn on the body. Using—or at least appearing to use—only materials available in the nineteenth century, many of these apparatuses sport surprisingly well-crafted wood and brass details and finishes. Even jewelry and accessories not treated as such in the actual period are sometimes decorated with faux timepieces, gyroscopes, gears, and springs as decorative objects. Goggles and wooden backpacks loaded with metal gizmos abound. Interestingly, all classes are represented in steampunk: from all levels of the nineteenth-century work-ing class—miners, blacksmiths, maids, and prostitutes—to the wealthy upper classes can be seen at a steampunk convention.

Another phenomenon of this period is the regular masquerading events that began to proliferate in larger cities, such as *Dances of Vice* in New York City, *Masquerade Events* in London, and *Carnevale Praha* in Prague, in addition to the private masquer-ade parties and events that seem to be increasing on Facebook and Internet searches. Performance-based costume events have begun to escalate in the early twenty-first century and allow appropriately costumed individuals to immerse themselves in an active fantasy of an imaginary life, frequently associated with a free space of sexual alliances and flirtations. What began as an adolescent practice of popular culture has become a highly nuanced practice of adults, perhaps seeking relief from the crushing demands of postmodern life. One of these celebrations of imaginary life has brought the Fetish Club—once the enclave of the secret and abject—into the realm of the fashionable pursuit. Clubs such as the famous KitKatClub in Berlin have become a destination for hipsters seeking exposure and prestige: the only requirement for the entrance is the fashionable fetish costume—the more revealing and darkly ominous the better. This era of the postmodern, positioned at the edge of the millennium, seems to mark a turning point in the progress of men's and women's fashions, as well as the transformation of the fetish from the despised and denigrated practice of "primitive" and marginalized people to a cultural paradigm of the postmodern.

–3–

Fetish Identity

The Question

Ultimately, one of the most provocative questions about the role of fetish in contemporary fashion is this: What happened, precisely, in the late nineteenth century that resulted in the adaptation and consequent transformation of women's underclothes into the fashions of fetish? This transformation occurred to the extent that these garments not only became the accoutrements of fetish, but also came to signify fetish so closely, so profoundly, that they in themselves, through their very presence, define fetish in contemporary culture. Critics, scholars, and historians all tend to circle the issue, sometimes approaching it but not quite all the way to the core. Yet it is of vital concern: how did the myriad threads forming the web of contextual events—such as low birthrates, medical and psychiatric interventions, the rise of fashion and markets, degeneracy, inversion, *masculinisme*, and erotomania (discussed earlier)—coalesce into an impulse, a drive, and, most critically, a stage upon which fetish performance developed using the humble underwear of women?

The answer seems to be as complicated as the question. It certainly is about modernity and its accompanying conditions of the commodified culture of bourgeois capitalism, its expanding and sophisticated technologies, markets, and processes; the utopian impulses that saw an aesthetic of purity, simplicity, universality, and masculine individualism develop; and above all, the emergence of the modern subject, in whose construction fashion has "seamlessly integrated the object into the individual subject."[1] As Lehmann explains,

> The subject-related, male mode of behavior dominating aesthetic perceptions in Romanticism is superseded by the object-related, female *la mode*, which symbolizes a changed society enamoured with progress and consumption as it does modern stylistic qualities . . . Women's fashion—that is, the objectification of the female—would flourish within establishment of an unqualified form of capitalist and patriarchal society, out to dominate the female sex.[2]

Yet in the paradoxical formation of nineteenth-century cross-dressing, we find a romantic rebellion against the strictures of this rigid patriarchal culture.

Fig. 3.1   An early twentieth-century photograph of two young women in costume—one cross-dressed as a young boy. This sort of costume play was not unusual in the early days of photography. Photo courtesy of Sarah Norris.

Cross-dressing: "The Figure that Disrupts"

The introduction of masculine-tailored riding jackets in women's fashion, juxtaposed with the exaggerated feminine symbology of the hourglass figure—idolized in both men's and women's clothing—was perhaps the most ironic manifestation and articulation of the creeping practice of cross-dressing, or transvestism, written about in the late nineteenth century by medical professionals and by critics. The eroticization of clothing had become part of the discussion that, on the surface at least, tended to respond to the still illegal wearing of trousers by women. However, "[m]ale transvestism . . . was portrayed relatively seldom, while female cross-dressing was an immensely popular theme."[3] Actresses and other demimondaines garnered considerable titillated attention and amusement as they dressed in men's clothes and, consequently, were the subject of many caricatures and works of erotic art. Yet men dressing as women was a deeply "closeted" practice, given that it profoundly threatened the albatross of Victorian bourgeois masculinity. As Anne McClintock explained, "Clothing became central to the policing of social boundaries . . . For this reason, the historical figure of the cross-dresser becomes invested with a potent and subversive power . . . the figure that disrupts."[4] Part of this "sumptuary panic" was to be laid at the door of the gender and sexual transformations emerging at this time. Freud, Binet, Kraft-Ebbing, and other medical and social scientists had begun to pick the scab that had occluded these ongoing transformations, and as a result, a flurry of writing began to address the erotic content of clothes.

Karl Kraus in his essay "The Eroticism of Clothes" from *Die Fackel* (1906), written just after the turn of the century, suggested that, in fact, what we eroticize is not the naked body under clothes; rather, because we experience the body clothed—that is, masked by coverings that disguise the "true shape and essence" of the wearer— what we eroticize is the gap between the clothes and the naked body. Further, he states that the differentiation of clothing for the genders is derived from the different lifestyles required by each, the development of which "signifies an important stage in the development of eroticism and opened up a boundless profusion of erotic possibilities."[5] One of those possibilities lay in the clothes worn by the "opposite sex." Perceiving the sexual binary between the genders to be defined by the heterosexual attraction to the other, Kraus suggests that as a sexual symbol (for men), women's clothes become fetishized, and male cross-dressing—which he designates a "favorite passion of the erotic play instinct"—serves as an enticement for male homosexuality; conversely, a woman in man's clothes is a manifestation of a "widespread" latent bisexuality. He elaborates in detail:

> The current resemblance of women's clothing to men's, the man's hat atop a female coiffure, the stand-up collar around a woman's neck, and the man's overcoat as female garb, arise from—as the erotic effect on the man who experiences it as "chic" or "piquant" proves—an unconscious bisexuality. Also deserving particular mention in this connection is the woman's trouser, invented for practical reasons but in its gradual configuration clearly revealing its particular suitability as an erotic fetish.[6]

Kraus's comments have a distinctly commercial tone, particularly as he objectifies the women's trouser through its "suitability as an erotic fetish" in service for male consumption. Indeed, the balance of the essay lays out in suspicious detail how the invention of underclothes and their luxurious fabrics produced the "fitted waist," which creates for the female wearer a "divided body" and gives the image of "an insect, a wasp." Furthermore, Kraus notes how "the hindquarters of the wasp hypnotize the eye of the male . . . [and that] the fetishism of the [female] buttocks (one of the strongest and most general manias of the last hundred years) has brought about the most wondrous fancies in women's fashion: the crinoline, the *cul de Paris* [bustle], and the corset."[7] And Kraus continues on, much like a carnival barker: citing the invention of tricolette—a thin fabric used for women's stockings—he regales how its construction and color "simplifies and isolates for the eye the form of the body";[8] transparent fabric and lace "blur or disarray" the body contours, creating an increased arousal as they "let nakedness glisten forth out of a delicate haze to make desire even more covetous of it."[9]

These extremely provocative, highly lascivious, and obsessively detailed descriptions of women's fashions and their materials by men attest to a fetishistic attachment. Yet how can we understand this obsessive interest in women's clothing? We must return to the dandy and the accompanying implications and effects of his hegemonic domination of men's clothing then and now. Baudelaire reminds us that "dandyism is a modern thing, resulting from causes entirely new—appearing when democracy is not yet all-powerful, and the aristocracy is just beginning to fall."[10] The harkening to the "new," a moniker of modernity, is an understatement on Baudelaire's part, for men's fashions in the years approaching the Revolution "marked the end of the vestimentary of the *ancien régime*, and the beginnings of a new liberty of dress."[11] More importantly, the new men's fashions marked the politicization of dress in France. Steele suggests that in the aftermath of the wrenching Revolution, fashion was highly variegated as the lower classes began to mingle with the aristocracy in the uneasy period of the Directory. Further, attempts were made "to design a new costume for French citizens"[12] so as to quell the underlying sense of social and political upheaval and impending chaos that lurks in the remarks of critics of the time. Chateaubriand in Paris remarked,

> Paris in 1792 no longer looked the same as in 1789 and 1790; this was no longer the revolution in its infancy . . . Variety in dress was a thing of the past; the old world was slipping into the background; men had donned the uniform cloak of the new world which as yet was merely the last garments of the victims to come.[13]

Chateaubriand was noting the radical political and demographic transition that became part of the paradigm shift into the modern. Looking "aristocratic" became dangerous. Yet the slovenly "plebian . . . recognized by their rags [and] bronzed complexions"[14] (who in fact were peasants from the south of France) were now mobile and coming into Paris as the class restrictions of the old world disintegrated, and the French struggled to comprehend the new world order, yet to be fully realized. What emerged was the frantic need to establish a male identity that could hold up the "virtues" of the banished aristocrat, a man who could show himself to be a man of the people and at the same time of fashion: the new male identity. And it is here that the seminal moment of fetish fashion begins to emerge. With the slow adoption of the British import of the dandy, the Revolution, in its "time of crisis for attire,"[15] brought forward issues of class and began to position fashion as the reified manifestation of those issues.

As a successful class interloper—a class "hero" if you will—Beau Brummel exemplified a new ideal for a population desperately seeking a masculine model who represented the aristocratic virtues without *being* an aristocrat. Despite not being of aristocratic birth—he was the son of Lord North's private secretary—Brummel "was able to transverse class," befriending the Prince of Wales, the future George IV, "who was a good bit older but impressed with Brummel's wit and dress." As a result of his friendship with the prince, Brummel came to be known "as a virtual oracle on matters related to dress and etiquette—virtually a court fashion arbiter."[16] Baudelaire noted this identity as "the last burst of heroism in the midst of decadence," yet this heroic mode signified the profile of the new modern male individual. That is to say, paradoxically, the dandy seemed instead the first burst of modern heroism in the midst of a chaotic, dying regime. He is the first fetishized superman of the modern era, as Lehmann explains beautifully:

> The fashionable attire was no longer a completely subjective statement, an extravagant display of wealth and status, but was subjugated to a general rule, to a moral code that declared the virtues of eschewing everything ostentatious, and displaying individuality through well-chosen details rather than grand gestures . . . Brummell reified Kant's categorical imperative in coining a standard attire that could act as a general law for the enlightened male, while retaining the significance of an individual sartorial maxim that would always appear to be integral to that law . . . reflecting a restrained simplicity to confront the increasing rapidity of change in contemporary life, it anticipates attitudinal patterns toward an emerging modern culture.[17]

Dandyism was the perfect move at the perfect time. It was a masquerade that allowed for a sophisticated indication of upper-class virtues yet, at the same time, denoted the rigid moral code of the emerging and powerful bourgeoisie; it signified masculinity as a sober, controlled, and singular uniform identity, and it also pointed to the "compliance with a new aesthetic experience that was—in a Kantian sense— 'disinterested.'"[18] In short, it changed forever the "gentleman" as an indication of class to a signifier of a moral position, part of whose baggage includes the values and prejudices of the aristocrat; meanwhile, it eschews class as an identity in favor of the projection of a unique moral individual. In fact, the dandy is ironic in that, despite primarily projecting uniqueness and individuality, he adopts a uniform that renders all indications of a unique identity *invisible*—except one: that of the modern man.

Adolf Loos, interestingly, asserted the "invisibility" of modern male fashion as the "correct" approach to dressing: " 'Rather, it is a question of being dressed in such a way that one stands out the least' . . . Thus to be dressed correctly one should go unnoticed in what Loos called 'the center of culture.'"[19] And Oscar Wilde agreed: "If one is noticed in the street, it means one is not well-dressed."[20] Loos explains that the fashionable and morally sound (male) citizen must concern himself with wearing the proper apparel in the proper surroundings, and the consequent need to "change his coat" from street to street "would not do." Instead, he establishes what will become increasingly and profoundly institutionalized in Western culture into the twentieth and twenty-first centuries: "[C]lothing is only modern when the wearer stands out as little as possible . . . on a specific occasion, in the best society."[21] So a respectful uniform, good for all occasions, is the proper, moral, and modern choice to make. This is to say that the modern man (for there is no other "modern" subject), as individual, acquiesces to the *category* of the modern to define the nature of his individuality. Surely, this is the heart of his "Great Renunciation": in renouncing "uniqueness"—not the same as individuality—he becomes the "mass man" of modernity, a stable and ordered identity beyond class yet sensitive to status, the status of the man of modern fashion. The Great Renunciation was a repudiation of the disorder and instability of a city of unique meanings, multiple origins, rapid advances of commercialism and consumerism, shifting values, and, most pertinent, the fear of indeterminate masculinity in exchange for the stable and ordered identity proposed by a uniform "uniform."

Yet Ulrich Lehmann notes that the goals of the dandy follow closely with the well-known traits of the modern: purity, abstraction, and universality. He states that the need for distinction, as opposed to uniqueness, "remains deeply embedded in modern urban society" and dominated modernity because it was an essential to "mutually excluding and approximating homogeneous spheres in an objectified heterogeneous society."[22] In other words, the need to be distinguished in a field of uniformed men was a deeply rooted aspect of modern masculinity, and rather than being a manifestation of class or aesthetics, it became a fairly complicated aspect of a "persistent struggle to construct an identity between subject and object, between thought and reality."[23] Lehmann speaks of the acceleration of the perception of time and philosophers' responses that begin to contextualize the culture:

> The new time consciousness . . . does more than express the experience of mobility in society, of acceleration in history, of discontinuity in everyday life. The new value placed on the transitory, the elusive and the ephemeral, the very celebration of dynamism, discloses a longing for an undefiled, immaculate and stable present.[24]

Deep within this cultural construct of time, realism became unhinged from its historical moorings and was set afloat as a concept in a sea of commercial and artistic innovations. It was a construct in which singular and long-stable identities of class and status frayed into multiple potentials and meanings, its historic manifestations shattering in a series of social, economic, and sartorial revolutions. Difference in gender, historically tied to reproductive and class meanings, became profoundly and absolutely marked through the demands of capitalism. In contrast to modernism's ideal of a stable, immaculate, and undefiled present, capitalism resulted in a cultural binary that juxtaposed an unstable remembrance and attraction to the past (embodied in female fashions) with an accelerated demand for the "new." The oscillations between the two positions developed a longing for stability, which some found through performance of the Other: in the cross-dressing of gender through the fetishizing of feminine underwear.

This rather surprising and improbable solution lies at the center of the maelstrom, in the persistent proclivity to attempt to construct an identity in the gap between subject and object and between the imagined and the performed identity. Fetish is a complicated relationship involving subject and object and, in this sense, an erotic relationship. According to the commentary of fetish practitioners, their fascination can originate as small children, as Freud asserted, but can also evolve in their experience as adults.[25] In attempting to identify the precise moment in which nineteenth-century women's underwear became such a durable and long-lasting set of fetishized objects (setting aside for the moment the considerable commentary of cultural critics, philosophers, psychologists, and psychiatrists), one needs to examine the condition of nineteenth-century experience. For although cross-dressing has long existed, in this particular time in Paris—this fin de siècle Paris in which so much was written about fetishism and cross-dressing—we might find a way to understand how this peculiarity happened.

McClintock reminds us, "Considerable theoretical rigor and subtlety are lost if all fetishes are reduced to the magisterial phallus . . . Instead of gathering these multifarious fetishes into a single primal scene, we might do better to open the genealogies of fetishism to more theoretically subtle and historically fruitful accounts . . . Since fetishes involve the displacement of a host of social contradictions [in different locations and times,] they defy reduction to a single originary trauma,"[26] suggesting "a more complex and historically diverse phenomenon."[27] Amanda Fernbach creates a more "complex and diverse" explanation of these types of trauma in her taxonomy of fetish types, which is based on the various ways of dealing with difference between subjects as well as the mode of disavowal of a particular lack and how its process of recuperation is manifested:

> *Classical Fetishism:* Makes the Other over in the image of the self, and disavows a "castration" (a phallically defined lack).
> *Pre-oedipal Fetishism:* Merges with the Other in a partial . . . or complete annihilation of the self . . . and disavows corporeal lack resulting from individuation by fantasizing reunification with a greater whole . . . or by disavowing death.
> *Decadent Fetishism:* Transforms the self into an image of Otherness, and disavows the cultural lack ascribed to marginal subjects.[28]

Cross-dressing and the fetish pursuits of the late nineteenth century, as well as current and more public fashion proclivities of the postmodern era, would seem to fall primarily into the category of decadent fetishism, though certainly Fernbach's other flavors of fetishistic behavior can be found in dungeons all over the world. As we enter into the moment of transformation, bear in mind this description is a play of an imaginary and singular moment, yet the reality was as vastly diverse as the subjects that experienced it.

Under the nineteenth-century patriarchy, "women . . . are figured not as historic agents but as frames for the commodity, valued for *exhibition* alone . . . in the iconography of modernity, women's bodies are exhibited for visual consumption."[29] And by the late nineteenth century, that visual consumption functioned as a mark of status for the middle-class male and the image of his power and status in the marketplace. Influenced by the departing aristocrats, an entire narrative of leisure and refinement had developed around the domestic scene, complete with happy children and a luxurious home piled high with commodities designed to overemphasize the gentility and status of the male purchasing power. As McClintock poetically explains, "Robbed of her productive labor, the middle-class woman became fitted, we are told, only for an ornamental place in society. There, drooping prettily in the faded perfume of watercolors and light embroidery, she lived only to adorn the worldly ambitions of her husband, the manufacturer, the city banker, the shipowner."[30] Although the reality undoubtedly did not match this idealized and commodified image of the genteel life of nineteenth-century middle-class women (since it sounds suspiciously like advertisement copy), class-conscious women across this culture nevertheless aimed to model their lives upon the idealized imagery, seeking approval and status among their peers and satisfaction in themselves in the only way open to them at this time. It was adopted by women whose goals had become adhered not only to her husband's but also to the imperatives of the society, the commodity market, and the consumer culture. McClintock suggests, "[A]part from the tiny, truly leisured elite—idleness was less a regime of inertia imposed on wilting middle-class wives and daughters than a laborious and time-consuming *character* role performed by women . . . Yet a housewife's vocation was precisely the concealment of this work."[31]

"The Scene Takes Place in a Delightful Boudoir . . ."[32]

One of the performative "scenes" that has come down to us in paintings, literature, and design as part of this idealized feminine world is the airless, bounded, and closeted world of the *boudoir*, where the magic transformation of women into the "wasplike" nineteenth-century enchantress takes place. Freud suggested that fetishism "has been relegated primarily to the 'private' realm of domestic space."[33] If we are to identify the moment of transformation of women's undergarments to fetish objects, we must acknowledge that it is the nineteenth-century bourgeois dressing room—real or imagined—that provided the stage, lights, and costumes of that transformation.

The boudoir is related to the female inner aspect—the secret potential of phallic power is the woman under the many layers of clothes. It was located in an inner sanctum of the cabinet, or *boudoir*—in French, the term means a woman's bedroom or private room but is formed from the eighteenth-century masculinist definition of *bouder*, "to sulk."[34] The implication is of an inner space of negative expression or embodiment, that is, a paraspace: a "bourgeois arrangement of space" that developed in the domestic structure, providing "zones forbidden to the opposite sex, such as the man's study, or *salle d'antiquitiés*, and the woman's dressing chamber . . . which served to render the cabinet a gendering divide within the interior."[35] This domestic space developed in the nineteenth century against the male-dominated exterior world of chaos and change in consumerism, class, and gender as a "smaller, more manageable world,"[36] which Apter describes thus:

> Often a simple room within the home, the fin de siècle cabinet, as a space in which assembled treasures nested and multiplied, habitually contained familial icons, *objets d'art* or private papers, themselves fetishized and invested with rarified forms of eroticism . . . seems to have merged with the newly minted sexual aberration of erotomania, itself appropriated and dramatically exploited by the "temple of love," from the courtesan's boudoir to the specialty house of prostitution . . . the cabinet became a consummate metonym for the *maison close* (literally, "closed house") . . . yoking the bourgeois notion of "home" to the morally tainted connotations of "closet" sexuality. As a spatial metaphor crisscrossing the high associations of connoisseurial collecting with the low associations of the prostitute's peep show . . . [it] demonstrates a disturbing set of slippages from object mania to erotomania, from household fetishism to brothel decadence.[37]

In much of the literature of the era, as well as the art, the "woman of the house" is "pictured" as yet another object for the domestic collection: "an erotic commodity or collector's item within the fin de siècle Imaginary," frequently analyzed in the future from the "masks or masquerades deployed to obscure her phallic deficiency (clothes, jewels, trinkets, maquillage, and so on)."[38] In many paintings, posters, caricatures, and (increasingly) photographs from the period, woman is "staged" as erotica, either as a straightforward prostitute or as the romanticized and idealized beauty of the domestic scene, with children hanging at her sides like cherubic angels in a Renaissance painting, or in a quiet moment after bath, or with friends—but placed within the boudoir. This presentation is nearly always positioned as a "peep" into the private interior world of the feminine. Yet even more contained within and nested into the Victorian spectorial structure is the *mise en abyme*—"composed as viewer-gazing-at-viewer-gazing-at-object-of-desire."[39]

For example, in Walter Ernest Webster's 1910 painting *The Glove* (Figure 3.2), a woman sits in her boudoir, gazing at an image of a Japanese geisha, the highly exoticized and orientalized symbol of allure of the time, who implied a feminine model of intelligence and talent as well as an independent potential sexuality. She has inadvertently—or intentionally—dropped her white glove, which sits beckoning on the floor at her feet. The glove, a prominent sexual symbol and fetishized object, dominates the painting. As we watch her gazing at the image, fanning the desire that has overheated her reddened cheeks, her ungloved hand pulls back her skirts as if to increase the visibility of the proffered glove. "Throwing down the glove," a phrase that has long indicated a challenge to engage in action, suggests a gesture toward an unseen

Fig. 3.2 Walter Ernest Webster, *The Glove*. Oil on canvas. One of many "boudoir paintings" created in this period. Courtesy of Peter Nahum at the Leicester Galleries.

suitor occupying the same position as the viewer. The glove—with its double indication of the phallic and the vaginal enclosure—suggests in its usage the sexual act, demurely indicated, delicately seductive. The subversive sense of passive availability juxtaposed with an eroticism that implies an innocent though coyly aggressive desire becomes part of the operative mechanisms of these boudoir paintings. The proposed unknowingness of the subject under surveillance usurps any responsibility for the eroticism of the moment, preserving the ideal purity—and ignorance—of a bourgeois womanhood that was configured increasingly through domesticity: "Conjugal domesticity and motherhood were gradually seen to offer the perfect molds within which to confine female sexuality and female authority."[40]

The boudoir became the place for private sexual intrigue—real or imagined. "[T]he boudoir was much more than a room: it generated discourse about sexual power relationships and was at the center of discussions about morality."[41] In this view, the male-defined room in which a woman could "sulk" and endure or, more appropriately, hide her blackest moments paradoxically becomes a private space of friendships—for lingering luxuriously out of the corset in light gowns or nude, sometimes for sexual encounters; sometimes it is the space of daughters and girl-friends playing "dress-up" in pastel colors framed by the classic props of this en-closed feminine cloister. In this place of a male-proscribed "dark mood," a radical subversion of the male prerogative is juxtaposed with the delicate fantasy of women and artists, and an enclosed, private, and manageable feminine "world" emerges. It is this alchemical condensation of various desires that produced erotomania and provided the energy for this transformation.

Dr. Ball, of the Doctors Moreau de Tours, Charcot, Magnan, and Ball from 1883 to 1887, wrote an article called "Erotomania or Erotic Madness" that consolidated all previous discussions of this convenient term into a singular "delusion projected by the subject into a living person often so remote that [it] . . . resembled an inanimate ob-ject or fetish-substitute," describing in enthusiastic detail how erotomaniacs "became *Fou par amour* or literally 'mad with love' tyrannically lording over their surrogate objects of desire or even attacking the beloved in the flesh."[42] Apter relates how many writers of this generation attached this maniacal behavior to the fad, adapted from eighteenth-century aristocratic pursuits, of collecting and obsessing over objects that increasingly became attached to the bourgeois woman: "Between its increasing 'feminization,' on one hand, and its resemblance to a secular cult, on the other, the high art of collecting was fast becoming a virulent petit-bourgeois sickness."[43] Soon it was not only identified as part of the homemaker's allure—"Let your nest be cozy, let us feel you in your thousand little nothings"[44]—but also began to be linked to the exotic lust of the prostitute, which, from the coded language of the previous quote, would seem to have been accepted widely. Apter links the obsessive, erotomaniacal collec-tion of objects with the boudoir, citing the work of Octave Uzanne, who according to Apter was—among other dubious titles—a writer of society, a historian of women's fashions, and a sociologist of prostitution. In his " '*Le Cabinet d'un Eroto-bibliomane*,' framed inside a larger work called *Les Caprices d'un bibliophile* (1878), he merged the medical codes of erotomania with the pornographic conventions of the closet erot-ica."[45] In this work, the collector/client/medical man within the brothel "becomes prey to the basest instincts, little better than the lust-stricken woman of easy virtue whose species he collects."[46] Linking the male/collector/subject with the female/prostitute/object located in the boudoir/brothel secures the boudoir in its sexual innuendo and sets up the scene for the next maneuver in the drama of the fetish fashion's origin.

Again it is Apter who makes the next step: "From this inadvertent fusion of collector and prostitute, subversive psychohistorical consequences arise: mascu-line changes places with feminine, prostitute becomes collector (of lovers), and the cabinet itself is gradually transformed into a not-so-secret museum of erotic curiosities . . . The double conversion of prostitute into collector and collector into prostitute"[47] is exposed as a *mise en abyme*, wherein the collector is caught in a closed rotation of having his own desires mirrored back upon himself. As he gazes upon the prostitute (or the bourgeois *hausfrau* in the character role of "the prostitute") as an object of desire, and she gazes back at him, simultaneously she is transformed into prostitute/collector-of-lovers and he is positioned as one of the lovers/objects of *her* desire. And it is this heated exchange that provides much of the dangerous allure and sexual excitement of the moment: "the provocative confession that the edicts of power are reversible."[48] Importantly, however, this little swiveling subversive scene is primarily an imaginary scene scripted by desires and projected into the cultural conception of the boudoir. It is precisely the potential of this imaginary scene with its exhilarating power shifts that fuels the boudoir paintings and caricatures appearing in vast numbers in this time.

Yet there is another layer of psychosexual mechanism at work in this scene: the power-shifting theater of sadomasochism, or, popularly, S/M. S/M emerged at the end of the eighteenth century, with Enlightenment reason and imperialism in its industrial form, composing a subculture "shaped around the ritual exercise of social risk and social transformation. As a theater of conversion, S/M reverses and transforms the social meanings it borrows."[49] S/M is a theater of exchanging roles and "playing" the Other, the scenes of which were—and are—taken from the transformations of industrial, imperialistic, class, gender, and racial subjects during times of radical and hegemonic changes; in the late nineteenth century, its scenes came from "the cult of domesticity and the cult of empire."[50] In the theater of the boudoir, it is a performance of gender, class, and power. This performance becomes an intimate, luxurious ritual, deeply dependent on the costumes and props of sexual allure and a Rococo femininity. As the forces of societal pressures of gender and class transformations bore down upon late nineteenth-century men and women, the theater of S/M provided a script through which an alternative—although theatrical and sadistic—is proposed to balance the rigors of their society. McClintock liberates the practice of S/M from its denigrated status by suggesting it as a "reality check" for societies under delusion:

> For Victorian science, nature was the overlord and guarantor of power . . . S/M enacts the male's "natural" sexual aggression and the female's "natural" sexual passivity . . . the outrage of S/M, however, is precisely its hostility to the idea of nature as the custodian of social power . . . Since S/M is the theatrical exercise of social contradiction, it is self-consciously *antinature* . . . in the sense that it denies the existence of natural law in the first place. S/M presents social law as sanctioned . . . by artifice and convention and thus radically open to historical change. S/M flouts social order with its provocative confession that the edicts of power are reversible.[51]

So now we have set the stage for our transformation of women's undergarments into fetish costume. We have the theater: the boudoir, rigged with S/M's power mechanisms of reversal. The characters enter as their rigid late nineteenth-century societal roles demand. First the dominant male/collector/"man-of-the-world"/*flâneur* enters, dressed in his dark three-piece suit with white starched collar and dark-colored tie. He is the "Hero of Modern Life." In fact, he is the sole modern subject, embodying all that modernity implies: the pinnacle of individualism, sober, detached, pure, rational, a standardized masculinity established by the power of the patriarchal engines of intellect, medicine, law, industry, and commerce. Supposedly he ejects all that is past for the projection of a new world empire, the old world of the past being decadent and weak. He is part of the modern masculine power bloc, identifiable by his uniform. Together they are all the same—like the pillars of the classical great white cultural and institutional architectures they have built in their own honor—but are also assured of their own individuality because the laws they have made say so. They know all the laws and the rules because they alone are the creators, responsible for the nation, the culture, and the empire.

Act I: He enters the boudoir with the fragrance of modern power and arrogant contempt still on him and sees the white kid glove lying beseechingly on the floor; he is surrounded by a theatrical rendering of the antimodern rococo past: the close, cloying soft pastel colors rich with the foreign allure of the feminine and *Japonisme*; fans; gilded mirrors; pale velvet revival rococo gilded chairs with soft pink shawls placed over the edge; and the great pile of satin trimmed in laces and velvets that forms the lower part of the wasp-woman, posed at her vanity as though she does not notice his entrance. She is embedded into and embodied within the set as an elaborate assemblage of pastel fragments, placed as the premium prop, the center of the scene, a historical set of objects vaguely coalescing as female and painted as a rococo aristocratic memory. She is wasp-shaped by a corset or (even more provocatively) without corset, her breasts bursting below the curls and "fascinators" framing her face; drenched in luxury, covered in layers of satins and petticoats, she shows a bit of ankle. She is the mistress of this domestic scene, the center of the view. She is positioned like an ornate spider in a complex web of rococo feminine props entirely devised for this performance of entrapment.

Act II: She—who will become codified as the dominatrix, "a figure who stands outside the norms of femininity"[52]—becomes the director who holds the script; and the male will now wait submissively, for his contempt has turned toward himself with his slavish desire, as he feels his need rise for this imaginary world focused on the past, for the warm, moist, uncontrollable body where "none of the ordinary rules apply,"[53] for this wealth of soft luxury with its taboo aristocratic insinuations, deep in the noir world of the feminine. She strip-teases him, with little whips of view, controlling the ebb and flow of his desire as she slowly removes the many layers of satins, silks, and velvets—down to the corset and her white knickers, her stockings and her boots. He knows that the terrifying nude body lies underneath these things, and these things—these remnants from the past, with all their decadence, their weaknesses, their ridiculous overloaded excesses—are yet deliciously and shamefully charged with orgasmic potential. He begins to fear and fantasize the forbidden and shameful feminine aspects of his own identity, which he is usually armored against in his quotidian existence by his *habit noir*. Now these underclothes of the female arouse a furtive recollection of his childhood memories of the female power of maternity, repressed through shame to the dark spaces of his psyche. McClintock suggests that

> in cultures where women are the child-raisers, an infant's identity is first shaped by the culture of femininity. After this initial identification with the mother, boys are then encouraged to identify away from the mother and their own incipient identities toward a masculinity that is "often abstracted and remote" . . . [It is] not founded on recognition of the self, but is formed through the negation of the feminine and that early founding identity.[54]

Act III: And thus women's underclothes of the late nineteenth century become the uniform of the Mistress and the dominatrix, the transgressive secret of the cross-dresser, and, in contemporary times, the ubiquitous costume symbolic of and associated with all fetish forms and fascinations. Though scripted here as a distinctly fetishistic scene from the demimonde, even heterosexual love scenes in popular cultures posit a powerful heroic male who loses his austerity and control over his body when the object of his desire takes control within the interior world of seductive heterosexual play. This highly theatrical scene is commonplace and "exaggerated to an almost cartoon aesthetic . . . played out again and again in many different forms. Its subversiveness is dependent upon its very theatricality, for by disclosing the artificiality, constructedness, and reversibility of relations of power and domination, these role-play games also manage to subvert them."[55] To all who have lived in modern Western popular cultures, it is so familiar as to be *naturalized* as normal; it is scripted under patriarchy as *the* modernist "seduction scene"—seen in theaters, films, and television, read in literature and pulp cultural forms. This scene is prevalent in Western culture, yet it is a further construction of early modernist S/M scenarios: "S/M plays social power backward, visibly staging hierarchy, difference and power, the irrational, ecstasy, and alienation of the body as being at the center of Western reason, thus revealing the imperial logic of individualism, but also irreverently refusing it as fate."[56]

And just what is this "imperial logic of individualism" that had so configured the male as the paradoxical lone individual subject, who identifies so strongly with a standardized uniform model of masculinity and control yet seeks this theater of power reversal? McClintock quoting Nancy Chodorow argues "that cultural patterns of childrearing give rise to different boundary experiences in males and females. In households where women are the primary caretakers, girls 'come to define themselves as continuous with others; their experience of self contains more flexible or permeable ego boundaries. Boys come to define themselves as more separate and distinct, with a greater sense of rigid ego boundaries and differentiation.'"[57] This would suggest that in nineteenth-century bourgeois France—and elsewhere in modernity—the strict division between genders had literally engendered the cult of individuality. Further, it implies that in making the distinction between subjects in a family a specifically gendered consideration, boys grew up apart from mother and sisters, developing a sense of self distinct from the females and their domestic milieu and looking to the men away from the home as a model for self and occupation.

Yet our modern man—a lone dog loping along in the exterior world of nation and commerce, automatically in competition with other men and judged constantly and severely on his ability to perform with an instrumental and calculating prowess— longs for the warmth and comforting world under the control of his mother and sisters. This is a world of automatic acceptance, of loving physical contact, of visual richness in preparing for guests, of cooking food in a warm kitchen, of cleaning and laundering with clothes fresh in the sunlight on the clothesline, of the feminine rituals of dressing while talking to others (it was common at this time that a woman would receive guests in her boudoir), which sealed in a sensual and sexual desire associated with the community of "women's work." But also, he was the son—the preferred gender in a culture that valued sons over daughters—and therefore was treated to particular and deferential attention and affection by the women in his bourgeois home. And it is precisely these mundane household tasks and the feminine identities of mother, sister, nurse, or maid that become the identities, objects, and narratives of fetish performance—both then and now: "By cross-dressing as women or as maids, by paying to do 'women's work,' or by ritually worshipping dominas as socially powerful, the male 'slave' relishes the forbidden feminine aspects of his own identity, furtively recalling the childhood image of female power and the memory of maternity, banished by social shame to the museum of masturbation."[58] Linking the enclosed world of the boudoir performance to masturbation, a sexual act usually performed by the subject alone (which went against the goal of the bourgeois sexual experience of family-building), pulls this performance into a dark theater of shame, where all such sexual acts and performances have been placed in modernity. This was indeed the behavior that Charcot, Binet, and other medical men of the time feared had led to homosexuality, impotence, and erotomania. Along with the governmental and societal mechanisms of nineteenth-century France, their shrill warnings and charge to "protect and punish" society brought about the very scripts of S/M narratives: "Punishment now lay in the visible representations of an abstract, bureaucratic power, which took the effect as a series of ritual restraints—detention, incarceration, regulation, restraining, restrictions, fines, and in some cases, rationalized and limited corporal punishment."[59]

Yet in the memory of the past, beyond the "new science" these medical and governmental men created, insight might be gained. McClintock emphasizes that "S/M is haunted by memory"; she further suggests that "by reenacting loss of control in a staged situation of excessive control, the S/Mer gains symbolic control over perilous memory," and by "reinventing the memory of trauma, S/M affords a delirious triumph over the past, and from this triumph, an orgasmic excess of pleasure."[60] I would suggest that it also can be precisely the *lack of control* and, more so, the lack of the need *to be in control* that provides the *jouissance*, the explosive orgasmic excess, brought on by the reenactment not necessarily of a traumatic memory but of idealized and romanticized memories of the bourgeois masculine childhood myth of the lives of women. In his memory, control is exerted not by the individual woman but by a consensual community of women in the closed and bounded world of bourgeois domesticity. They performed tasks based in a sensual and material world, which had the effect on his observing psyche of positive, knowable, and satisfying occupations that rendered closed results—cleaning him, feeding him, and comforting him—which were somewhat irrelevant to the larger, more abstract and instrumental tasks of the industrial, commercial, and governmental world. In this mythic world, mother's punishment—perhaps less harsh than father's—brought into focus his lack of responsibility and his free pass ("boys just being boys") to be bad without much retribution, and perhaps there was a subtextual parental relief at the assurance that he was "all boy." This is all to say that I suspect there is not one simple origin story of the fetishizing of gender performances but instead a multitude of highly nuanced, very particular responses to imposed gender restrictions and demands—"a parody of authority, a challenge to it, a recognition of its secret, sexual nature"[61] forcing the individual psyche into the creation of his own narration, his own theatrical play whose "climax" comes at a moment of his own devising.

Judith Butler's now famous dictum emphasized gender as a performance that is not derived from natural sources but constructed entirely of precisely these sorts of cultural imperatives:

> Butler proposes a performative gender, a set of repeated bodily acts that in their execution constitute the very identity they purportedly express. A gendered identity is thereby . . . a post-facto fabrication that regulates an individual's corporality and channels it into discrete gender categories . . . however . . . performing one's gender is neither an individual matter nor an existential freedom. It must be negotiated within the constraints of a patriarchal power structure that aligns sex, gender, and desire in accordance with the strictures of a compulsory heterosexuality.[62]

So our modern man is not only performing the cross-dressing role of the maid in a fetish performance, for example, but he also—and with almost no knowledge of doing so—is performing "modern man" and even "man" himself. In contemporary times, this notion of man is also generally accepted as the "natural" manifestation of people with a penis, yet it is a hand-me-down (to use the sartorial phrase), a gender identity fresh from the vintage store of history that, despite a few adjustments because of age, seems to still fit. Butler, in her discovery, appears to suggest that gender performance can be a nested set—like a Russian doll: if "the anatomy of the performer is already distinct from the gender of the performer, and both of these are distinct from the gender of the performance, then the performance suggests a dissonance not only between sex and performance, but sex and gender, and gender and performance . . . *In imitating gender, drag implicitly reveals the imitative struc-ture of gender itself—as well as its contingency.*"[63]

Yet perhaps the most significant insight gained comes through the power transfers that accompany and are highlighted in this theatre of gender: that power itself, like gender, is also an artificial construction—not a natural manifestation of privilege or birth. It is revealed through fetish performance to be contingent, constructed, and "sanctioned neither by fate nor God, but by social convention and invention, and thus open to historical change."[64] Modernism brought about a radical separation of the genders into two extremely stereotypical roles, which were strictly determined and obsessively critiqued by their sartorial inscriptions.

Postmodern Fetish Theory: A Lesson from Mulvey

How do we understand fetish in a culture that has undeniably taken a radical turn from the modern into a contemporary postmodern moment of profound technologi-cal advances that have altered the very basis of culture and communication? The transformation was so profound that it was frequently described with a series of binary adjectives set in opposition to the modern culture: modern/postmodern, high culture/popular culture, industrial/technological, center/margins, singular/plural, and so forth. The most provocative yet essential element in this discussion lies in a trans-formation that defied a simple binary opposition: the troubling relations between objects and subjects in the popular culture, which have become a series of sliding signifiers that cloud the once clearly defined order of social relations. To articulate the specific transformations that fetish theory performs in the postmodern period, I will use some elements of an essay written in 1993 by feminist cinema theorist Laura Mulvey, titled "Some Thoughts on Theories of Fetishism in the Context of Contemporary Culture,"[65] as a foundation on which the various postmodern theo-ries tend to be based. That foundation lay in the two great theories of fetish of the previous century: Freud's psychoanalytical theory and Marx's economic theory. She suggests that these two theories, despite the differing perspectives extending from them, also converge on central aspects that, in so doing, inform contemporary theories:

> The obvious link between their concepts of fetishism is that both attempt to explain a refusal, or blockage, of the mind, or a phobic inability of the psyche to understand a sym-bolic system of value within the social and the psychic spheres . . . the Marxist concept is derived from a problem of inscription: that is, the way in which the sign of value is, or rather fails to be, marked onto an object, a commodity. It is in and around the difficulty of signifying value that commodity fetishism flourishes. The Freudian fetish . . . [is] constructed from an excessive, phantasmatic inscription: that is, the setting up of a sign, which is of value only to its worshippers, to conceal a lack, to function as a substitute for something perceived as missing.[66]

Thus, in the Marxist concept, the sign of value (labor) cannot attach itself and so floats unattached to the object as a commodity. In the Freudian concept, however, the sign of value is overvalued as a substitute for a specific set of subjects and floats in signification because of its imaginary and phantasmagorical nature, these subjects are trying to mask the lack that is implicitly present in their apprehension of social relationships. Both of these theoretical objects float: their attachment to their referents is vague and insubstantial, a thing of symbolic rather than perceptual performance, detached from the real—one because the labor that created it is invisible to the point of a magical imagined origination (particularly in fashion), and the other because the referent is a psychic and imagined ghost of an object, a masked symbol of loss (particularly in fetish).

Mulvey spends the bulk of her discussion attempting to understand these two theoretical albatrosses—that of Marx and Freud—both of which swivel around the part that "inscription" plays in determining the signification or meaning of objects in the social exchange of signs of value through their referential function. Interestingly, Mulvey intends this discussion as an "experiment," usually considered a tentative endeavor that does not posit a clear and specific answer, but instead, she uses the play of different notions and insights gained from following the trail of signifiers that occur in the process. That is, she will follow the "symptoms"—a trail of bread crumbs if you will—expressed through popular cultural objects and left in the path of history (cinema in her case—fashion in ours). We do this to decipher and perhaps establish a mode in which these two theories might, in the play between their inscriptorial and semiotic linkages of sliding and free-floating signifiers, establish the foundation for why fetish has so profoundly influenced fashion design in the recent postmodern era.

A compelling, important point is the notion of the "rich sight," or spectacle, which refers to the power of the image and the difficulties in how to read that "rich sight." It is a notion that has followed us since the opening of the new department stores in nineteenth-century Paris, with their great open spaces, merchandise laid out in aisles in piles of color, and the promise of infinite choice. It was a "rich sight"—an image of plenty that had little to do with actual potential of the consumer, who even while knowing it was impossible to own yet still "owned" the image and felt it to be part of a fulfilling sense of self. In postmodern fashion, it is the "rich sight" of (as one example) Alexander McQueen's shows, with their massive baroque wealth of layered rich fabrics, giant flowing skirts, feathers, and ornate headdress displayed in a parade on a huge scale, exotic music completing the sight. Mulvey quotes Dana Polan: "[S]uch spectacle creates the promise of a rich sight, not the sight of particular objects, but *sight itself* [emphasis mine] as richness, as the ground for extensive experience."[67] The rich sight offers a signification without a referent: it is an image that we consume—not clothes or accessories, but an image of the performance of a narrative that has no referent, only the visual richness of commodities and the *jouissance*—the sexual or sensual ecstasy or pleasure we experience in this extreme rich sight that is characterized by explosiveness, dissipation, and the sense of a shattering of limits.[68]

Into this most postmodern of experiences, Mulvey suggests the tactic of *disavowal*, that is, "the mechanism, or mode of defense, invoked in fetishism, whereby the subject refuses to recognize the reality of a traumatic perception. Behind every incredulous spectator (who knows the events taking place are fictional), lies a credulous one (who nevertheless wishes these events to be true)."[69] As we watch the McQueen show, we believe in the sense of fullness and *jouissance* of the show—the dream of the fantasy landscape of beauty, wealth, and power—and at the same time, we know we will not ever have it . . . or will we? And it is here in this sliding signifier, this overwhelming postmodern experience of a twinkling unspeakable potential, that we apprehend the dramatic hold on the fetishist, so incomprehensible to older generations watching the young in their cultural pursuits. Mulvey explains it this way:

> Psychoanalytic film theory has argued that mass culture can be interpreted symptomatically, and that it functions as a massive screen on which collective fantasy, anxiety, fear, and their effects can be projected. In this sense, it speaks to the blind spots of a culture and finds forms that make manifest socially traumatic material through distortion, defense, and disguise. The aesthetic of the "rich sight" has lost touch with that delicate link between cause and effect, so that its processes of displacement work more in the interests of formal excitement and the ultimate denial of reference than as a defense against it.[70]

Yet she warns that in this wandering through the visual landscape of excess, the disavowal of lack and the henceforth attachment to the fetish can create "blind spots" that move the signification farther away from the problem of reference. She acknowledges that these commodified elements in images can create "bridges" to other sets of elements and, further, that the consequent "connotations, resonances, significances can then flow . . . between things that do not, on the face of it, have anything in common."[71]

That is to say, if we posit fetishism as a major structure of the postmodern condition, then within that structure, the various objects and their aspects become linked through disavowal; rather than confronting a block of referential "blind spots," fetishism instead creates a system whereby the commodity market is supported by the psychoanalytic disavowal linked to a lack that the culture *as market* supports. "The formal structures of disavowal create a conduit, linking different points of social difficulty and investing in 'sight' as a defense against them,"[72] and those investments create a certain energy for fetish production and consumption that circulates through the economic system as it both is generated by and benefits from the psychoanalytical fetish construct of disavowal.

This creates a sort of cultural surface or texture formulating an aesthetic of visual excess and lack of depth, which is concomitant with the symptoms of postmodern culture. Yet I would suggest that there is a tinge of yearning for that depth, which emerges in nostalgia and haunting of past forms—particularly in fashion. Caroline Evans cites the way in which fashion shows of the late twentieth and early twenty-first centuries

> were haunted by earlier visions . . . Christian Dior's Autumn-Winter 2000–1 haute couture collection spun a fantastical narrative on an imaginary correspondence on fetishism between Freud and Jung, playing out the perverse secrets of an Edwardian family in pictures on the catwalk . . . Like the work of psychoanalysis which recalls the ghosts of the past in order to exorcise them in the present, the finale piled up memories out of sequence, bringing the past into the present.[73]

Paradoxically, in the late nineteenth century, it was these very "ghosts of the past"— the *habit noir* and the Victorian gowns—that occluded the instability of individuals' gender with the definitive masking of uniforms that precisely inscribed gender and gender role in the culture and on the individual body. In the late twenty-first century, the pastiche of these very forms in the fashions of both genders has brought into knowledge and discourse the contemporary instability of genders under a persistent patriarchy. Fashion in the postmodern era, then, provides a screen, a surface much like the cinematic screen, which not only erases its "mechanics of production" but also supplants them with the mechanics of fetish production; it also matches their disavowals in an imaginary and symbolic performance of a mythic past in which genders were imaginarily secured and beauty was linked to gender role through clothing forms. Mulvey states,

> This duality of structure facilitates displacements so that images and ideas that are only residually connected—fascination with [gender] as surface and [fashion] as surface— can slide together, closing the gap between them like sliding doors. The topography of the phantasmatic space acts as a conduit for shifts in signification . . . Between femininity and commodities as seduction and enigma, with both premised on appearance fashioned as desirable, and implying and concealing an elusive unknowable essence.[74]

Mulvey suggests that "cinema finds its most perfect fetishistic object, though not its only one, in the image of woman."[75] She argues for the primacy of the female form in the mechanism of the fetish masquerade; certainly eroticism and all its connotations for the body have been scripted as a feminine domain in a dual cipher, as commodity and as vehicle containing the *objet á* (the lost object of original *jouissance*, the holder of desire), as signified by her costume. Her body becomes the department store: the site of multiplicity and of the "rich sight," the promise of youth, desire, plenty, and beauty as "an artful incognito designed to prolong the male viewer's distraction from the absorbing prospect of a hypothetical female phallus."[76] This artful incognito as fetish form was and is a caricature of feminine sexuality—especially in the eighteenth and nineteenth centuries but also in the postmodern age—with the essential areas of eroticism and potential penetration that were, and are, blown out of proportion or made salient through various clever sleights of hand (through labor) and eye (through a gaze of desire).

But it is not all for male satisfaction. Freud, Otto Rank, Joan Copjec, and Apter all allude to a narcissistic effect on what Copjec calls a "sartorial superego" for the female that as a result of this effect, emerges and "assimilates fetishism into narcissism and in the process takes away many of narcissism's pejorative connotations."[77] As Mary Ann Doane further points out,

> [In] the tautological nature of the woman's role as consumer: she is the subject of a transaction in which her own commodification is ultimately the object . . . therefore the deflection of any dissatisfaction with one's life or any critique of the social system onto an intensified concern with a body . . . The body becomes increasingly *the* stake of late capitalism. *Having* the commodified object—and the initial distance and distinction it presupposes—is displaced by *appearing,* producing a strange constriction of the gap between consumer and commodity.[78]

This condition of both being and having the desired object swivels in a very satisfactory way for the fashionable female: in dressing "for success" as it were, the female body can serve as the hanger upon which her masked identity—among her many choices—hangs. Through acknowledging her position as a commodity in the social market, she occludes any shortfalls of expectation, accentuates her desirability, and enhances a narcissistic sexual titillation and, most significantly, the thrilling sense of power that extends from being the object of the gaze and therefore the controller of the view. The positive appraisal of her performance in this "anaclitic, purely supportive social body describes . . . the dependency of the female masquerader on a masculine social gaze that mandates the subordination of the female body, but [also] . . . prepares the ground for redefining the notion of 'support' as an anchoring, stabilizing ontology for the female subject."[79] This suggests that the female masquerader—whether a male or a female performer—is utilizing the highly fetishized mask of the popular cultural construction of the desirable woman as a commodity form (for there are other possible roles in the wardrobe of the feminine) for the purchase of power through desire.

Mulvey ends the essay by acknowledging that Hollywood has utilized this oscillation in the split between what we know and what we believe: "'[T]he aesthetics of fetishism,' however, derive from the structure of disavowal in the Freudian model ('I know very well, but all the same . . .'), which creates an oscillation between what is seen and what threatens to erupt into knowledge,"[80] that is, between knowledge and belief in potential. We gaze at the screen with rapt attention and insert our psyches into the narrative. By insertion, we agree to "buy into" the reality proposed because we desire the experience within the narrative that we know we cannot actually experience, but we hunger to believe it might be possible to experience because of the intensity of the narrative fiction. In film, as well as in all media and particularly in

fashion media, even quotidian experience of the same sort of event pales in compari-
son to the fictionalized construction wherein those elements that intensify emotional,
sexual, or sensual experiences are focused on, within a heightened but *believable*
contextual setting.

Mulvey and other critics suggest that this is the postmodern condition. Due to
the accelerated visual capacities of the "rich sight" offered by the Internet and other
technologies, the technologically altered experience of the visual has developed a hegemonic and fetishistic position in contemporary culture: "[T]his trompe l'oeil effect
is central for postmodern aesthetics, which came ultimately to use self-referentiality,
intertextual reference, and direct address in the interests of a pleasurable destabiliz-
ing of perception."[81] "Spectacle proliferates," Mulvey admonishes, as fetish in contemporary communications, masking over not only the realities of its complex and
highly mediated production but also the realities of the historical condition of the
culture that has produced the spectacle.

Yet even as the postmodern accepts and even celebrates the fetishized condition
of culture, fetish appears as an acknowledgment of the processes in play: fetish becomes a celebration of the gap between what is known and what is believed and forms
a performance of desire through its debatable ontological status. Questions appear
about how perception—whether of the real or of fiction—is comprehended in the mind
as "experience," both differentiated and understood. Both assume visual scenes as an
image in the mind, though originating in different realms. Extremely realistic aspects
of a contextual reality, rendered by technological and market means, blur the distinction between what is experienced as real and what is experienced as fiction. Evidence
is procured through the many profound attachments to popular cultural fictions and
media by subjects—and particularly by fan subjects—of the postmodern, who have
accepted the fetishized fictions of the postmodern as a mediated and experiential reality, despite the "I know very well . . ." condition of the negotiation. Many of these
subjects are from marginalized populations, whose participation in the mainstream
"realities" have been occluded as unacceptable through some aspect of their being,
whether that obstruction is real or perceived as real by the subject; again, the issue
of the ontological status of experience is at the heart of the postmodern condition.

This question of the ontological status of experience was visible in the films produced in the early decades of the postmodern era: *Being John Malkovich* (1999), *Inception* (2010), *Memento* (2000), *Pandorum* (2009), *Altered States* (1980), and all the
cyberpunk films of David Cronenberg, but in particular *Videodrome* (1983), emphasized the increasing suspicion that the status of experience was being blurred through
technological interventions into lived experience. This slippage also extended into
all aspects of the culture and developed rapidly as the potential for liberatory change
for marginalized subjects began to be acknowledged in popular culture, particularly
as it concerned gender and sexual identities. This much-discussed "blurring" aspect
referenced in relation to postmodern gender and identity positions is most visible in
the fashion scene as it traversed the postmodern rupture from the modern.

–4–

Fetish Style: Fetish as Fashion

If the penis were the phallus, men would have no need of feathers or ties or medals.

Eugénie Lemoine-Luccioni, *La Robe*[1]

Without the requirement suggested above that the penis be the phallus by Lemoine-Luccioni, we turn to those fetish costumes so celebrated, so deliciously transgressive, that they are found in the titillating images of furtive looks in dicey magazines and websites. That is to say, we will now look to the "feathers, ties, and medals" of contemporary fetish fashions to examine and discern how desire was and is demonstrated in the sartorial expression of the fetish performer. Though fetish remained deeply marginalized and relegated to low-level publications during the bulk of the twentieth century, the postmodern period brought a rise of popular cultural inclusion and celebration of fetishistic performance personalities, such as Leigh Bowery, Boy George, Michael Clark, Divine, and Betty Page; also influential was the popular rock music scene with, among others, the metal bands, glam bands, and Japanese visual kei bands, whose acts were defined by the extreme costumes they wore. Madonna's book *Sex* (1984) was also one of the first indications that fetish was coming out of the closet, resurrected from the dark margins of modern culture and voguing in its postmodern fashion forms as they had evolved from the late nineteenth century into the light of day.

In order to study the fashion of fetish, we must first untangle the vocabulary around clothing, fashion, and costume to clarify exactly how these objects are structured in social exchange and have been coded for meaning in the culture. This is not an exercise in academic form but rather the recognition of a need to convey how these forms have evolved from costume to fashion and the cultural ramifications they imply. It is because of the transition from costume to fashion that fetish was included in this series of books on subcultural fashion, and including such a profoundly repressed yet essential aspect of modern culture into fashion discourse changes the very nature of this distinct culture. As Rauch suggests,

The substitution of fashion for art in modernity . . . is predicated on the aesthetic appearance which both fashion and art have in common. Fashion unites people in time, in a newly visibly ideal, keeping society artificially in place which—tradition being lost— would otherwise disintegrate. Fashion allows the individual to be contemporaneous with the social system, a system whose defects and historically heterogeneous fragments are covered up by fashion . . . The more short-lived an era, the more it is oriented to fashion.[2]

Clothing, of course, refers to "garments in general,"[3] without qualifying conditions or categories, and it is perhaps as close to a neutral term as possible. Yet it still carries connotations of potential distinctions between clothed/civilized and unclothed/primitive subjects, therefore resurrecting colonial aspects that have long been part of the Western historical discourse. *Costume*, on the other hand, refers to

> [d]istinctive forms of clothing, including official or ceremonial attire such as . . . theatrical dress. The use of ornament preceded the use of protective garments; its purpose was to emphasize social position by a great display of trophies, charms, and other valuables . . . The term *costume* also includes accessories, such as the shoe, hat, glove, corset, handkerchief, fan, umbrella, cane, and jewelry; styles of wearing the hair . . . and beard; and primitive methods of body-marking and attaching ornaments to the body.[4]

This description represents clothing that is created for specific events, positions, and purposes. Currently, it is most associated with theatrical clothing—clothing that is symbolic of a specific character being played by an actor. In general terms, in the creation of that character, the actor and the costume can become conflated semantically through the process of dressing for performance in that "putting on the character" becomes synonymous with "putting on the costume." The costume, in its potent and subtle power to represent the identity of the character, is made up of those elements that foreground aspects of character but in an exaggerated form, in essence calling out qualities recognized by the popular culture as representing a particular quality or character. The more accessories and detail to the costume, the more complex and compelling is the denotation of character. In some cases, particularly in film and television advertising, the costume is so potent that it will "stand in" for the character, such as the bowler hat and the furled umbrella of the character John Steed in the popular television series *The Avengers* (1960–1969), which not only stood for the character but eventually came to stand for the entire series.[5]

In fetish performance, the costume in most senses is even more directly indicative of the character role. In this particular cultural phenomenon, the explanations for how fetish works depart from Freudian and other theorists' notions: the fetish "object"—or that which is fetishized—is no longer centered in an object but becomes narrativized in a play of character roles and actions. A memory or dream of a social scene in which the participant is the star becomes fetishized. This participant's erotic imagination has constructed a specific scenario of sexual satisfaction in which the real condition is supplanted by a play, a costumed performance that enacts his (and sometimes, though less often, her) erotic desire as actualized phantom identities and roles. We can observe this same effect of costume when people—especially children—slip on a Halloween costume, whether Dracula mask or sexy little black cocktail dress, a ballerina costume or a military uniform; the wearer, unaccustomed to that social role, whirls around, miming character actions, gesturing and playing in an improvised and caricaturized performance based in cultural meanings and associations. The costume—particularly in S/M—propels the actor into an imaginary scene that develops its context around the character—providing the set and scenery for the projection of the character through the subject's assumption of the costume, what we will later discuss as a condition of the *transversal*.[6] With that assumption, that "putting-on of the character," the subject not only is coerced to perform but—I would suggest—slips into and assumes the very identity of that character. Yet as the phallus figures as the object to be gained or at least negotiated in this performance, Garber asks, "Why is fixation on the phallus not called a fetish when it is attached to a man? The concept of 'normal' sexuality, that is to say, of heterosexuality, is founded on the naturalizing of the fetish. And this is dependent upon an economics of display intrinsic both to fetishism and to theatrical representation."[7]

This satisfaction derived from such play is evident in the proliferation of costumed events in all cultures and all times. The fetishist in his reenactment of his erotic scene derives an even more comprehensive satisfaction because, in fetish performance, he has the dominatrix to assist him in the completion of his scene, and he gains additional *jouissance* from being the "producer" of the play. He has "full control over the fantasy or situation. As playwright, director, and leading actor, the 'victim' actually determines the kind, degree, and duration."[8] In addition, the costumes themselves in fetish play are redolent with the form and fabric of fetish desires, doubling the erotic effect in the performer: he both wears his fetish and sees it mirrored back to him through the props and players in the enactment of his scene. This description recalls the Lacanian description of the "Imaginary," part of Lacan's schema of subject development:

> The Imaginary is a dimension in which the human subject's relation to himself, and to other people, is structured like, and by, his relation of his mirror image: a dyadic, symmetrical complementarity (whether between child and mirror or between child and mother) based on the fiction of a stable identity, a wholeness, which the mirror instates by equating self with an *image*.[9]

Unlike other dramatic or theatrical modes, fetish play is highly dependent on the image of the costume—whether in the form of clothing or apparatus—for the desired effect. Costume is the adhesive that binds the performance to the fetishist's dream; it adheres to his body through sight, sound, and touch and allows him to vault his imaginary erotics into a reality that is mediated by yet upheld through the particular slippery phrase of the fetishist: "I know, nevertheless . . ."

But in postmodernity, we have taken fetish costume performance out of the dungeon and into the mainstream and highly visible category of fashion. Where costume begins our understanding of the fetish play and serves as the mechanism for the assumption of character and identity, *fashion*, on the other hand, refers to

> [a]ny mode of dressing or adornment that is popular during a particular time or in a particular place (i.e., the current style). It can change from one period to the next, from

generation to generation. It serves as a reflection of social and economic status, a function that explains the popularity of many styles throughout costume history; in the West, courts have been a major source of fashion.[10]

Fashion also, as Rauch explained earlier, "allows the individual to be contemporaneous with the social system," using its cultivation and embedded status through the massive industry that has evolved during its history of increased commodification and corporatization since the late eighteenth century. But especially in terms of its use in this discussion, fashion refers to the combination of these definitions into a concept that includes not only its specificity to time and place, but also its position as an object of a capitalist and highly commodified culture; its unique place in the design business as the source of new color palettes, materials, and forms; and its mainstream manifestation not as objects of clothing as much as objects of publication and photography. Fashion, in short, has quietly assumed a hegemonic position in contemporary culture, arranging our objects into social categories and expectations and colonizing media.

Fetish Fashions

Introducing this collection of contemporary fetish fashions and their creators requires some description of their unique sexual fascination for the fetishist. Although the previous discussion has focused on the fetish performance—in clubs and in private—the center of the fetish condition lies in the subject's obsessive sexual relation to an object: "Inanimate object fetishes can be categorized into two types: form fetishes and media fetishes. In a form fetish, the object and its shape are important, such as high-heeled shoes. In a media fetish, the material of the object is important, such as silk or leather."[11] Because of the specific active sexual attraction that these objects hold for the fetishist, the collection—to use the fashion sense of the term— was developed over time in fetish communities and clubs. However, this does not in any way exhaust the potential fetishistic attraction of any object for a fetishist. In forums online and in interviews, the range of obscure and quotidian objects that have become fetishized is stunningly inexhaustible: from beach balls to vinyl cleaning gloves, virtually any object can be fetishized for sexual satisfaction. There are as many reasons and stories of origination as there are fetish objects, and although some experiences happened as children, many others came as surprises in adulthood. One interviewee—a babyist, or infantilist—explained its power this way: when you experience that founding sexual moment in contact with that object or scene (in his case), that initial orgasmic event is so powerful, so "blindingly intense," that for the rest of your life, you must seek to repeat it again and again by endlessly re-creating the moment through the use of the object or the fetish performance.

In discussions with the remarkable Mistress Jean Bardot,[12] I was able to learn how each of the components of traditional fetish fashions operates in terms of physical sensations and phantasmic identifications in the fetish performance. To consider these specifications, each object will be discussed under the heading of its primary performative aspect: *constriction, character*, and *effectuation*. Of course, any category also may be involved in the other aspects, but each of these aspects seems to address a certain predominant position in the alchemy that is the fetish transformation for certain objects. In addition, fetish designers whose work is exemplified by these objects will be discussed and highlighted.

Constriction

Fetish clothing objects that constrict were also described by words like "encasement," "restriction," and "immobilization" by Mistress Jean in her discussions on how these elements of fetish fashions work for the fetishist in performance. John Money suggests, "Fetishes can be classified as related either to haptic, or olfactory imagery in perception of fantasy. Haptic pertains to the feeling of pressure, rubbing, or touching."[13] Haptic elements tend to hold the body into itself tightly through the compressed construction of the media involved. Key categories are the various corset objects (torso, penis, neck, arms, hands, legs). *Zentai*[14] or skinsuits, thigh-high boots, bondage straps, stockings, gloves, and a new object of high technology, the balloon suit, are all additional garments that can create the same constricting sensation. Each effects a constriction on the body that at the very least heightens sexual feeling and, at the most, helps the wearer achieve an orgasmic climax when encased and embraced tightly by the garment. This happens in at least two ways: in clinging tightly to the skin, the suit heightens not only a sensual and erotic awareness of the skin, but also the sense of the body underneath the skin: the muscles, nerves, and bone structure, particularly in movement. As Louise J. Kaplan explains, "The epidermis-dermis skin then becomes a two-sided surface that faces inward toward the brain and other organs, nerves, and muscle inside the body and outward toward the external world."[15] Secondly, it is precisely this outward look to the world beyond that creates the particular phenomenon of the "body image," which develops as part of the intricate mechanism of embodiment. This body image forms as a consequence of being conscious, as an embodied subject enmeshed in social relations; Kaplan portrays this phenomenon as a Möbius strip formation that twists around to touch every part of the body, then spirals around, bringing the inside surface outward[16] and linking the two sensations in a dance of erotic consciousness. The notion of a mirrored image of the self—whether actual or imaginary—comes into play as the sensual awareness of the subject is brought to the skin and its delicate sensory network, creating an image of the embodied self that forms as a phantom continuously haunting the conscious subject in the social world:

> Our body image, a mental or psychological out growth of having a skin that transports erotic vitality to the rest of the body . . . Though it tends to unify tactile, postural, kinesthetic, visual, and aural sensations, the body image is also capable of dispersal,

disruption, dissolution, and disunity. The body image is immensely pliable, intensely suggestible, and amenable to all varieties of biological, psychological, and social trans-formations of the actual physical body.[17]

The body image and its power in the formation of subjectivity and identity are stimu-lated by the sensation of constriction, which brings the image into an intense con-sciousness for the fetishist. This contemporary constrictive category in garments had its birth in the nineteenth century "tight-lacing," a type of constriction that was achieved through the use of various kinds of corsets. As Steele notes, "Michel Fou-cault reminds us, the body has been subject to various kinds of 'disciplinary power.' The relations of power 'invest it, mark it, train it, torture it, force it . . . to emit signs.'"[18] Though tight-lacing was used in earlier centuries as an aesthetic device to narrow the feminine waist, the burdens of the nineteenth century discussed earlier had delivered a discursive and "marked" change around the corset from a mere gar-ment to a "disciplinary" and "training" device for young women especially. Enor-mous numbers of medical articles, caricatures, critical reviews, pornography, and testimonials were published about the corset in the latter part of the century.

Both David Kunzle and Valerie Steele give excellent accounts of the obsessive and curious published discourse around tight-lacing—those "emited signs" of so-cial, political, and medical/scientific hysteria around the corset and its tight-lacing functions—and consequently, they will not be repeated here. Michel Foucault also reminds us that areas "where the grid is tightest, where the black squares are most numerous, are those of sexuality and politics."[19] Instead, a discussion of tight-lacing and the desire for constriction in terms of the body will reveal how the majority of fetish costumes function in creating various sexual and psychic responses. At the root of the desire for constriction is the desire for boundaries, and specifically boundaries that expand into a series of inner and outer, psychic and physical markers that contain, confine, and define within the fetish fantasy and the realm of S/M—and specifically masochism. Lyn Cowan describes the process in this way:

> Physical enactment of a masochistic fantasy gives shape and body to the fantasy, while the contract [of the fetishist: "I know, nevertheless . . ."] holds it firmly within bounds of the imagined world . . . which heightens the limitations, the bondage, the punishment by giving them specificity . . . Once shame has moved into memory, its experience is fixed timelessly, implacably, mortared in humiliation, cast in masochistic remembrance, a permanent monument.[20]

Cowan is tracking the origin of masochistic desire, acknowledging the place of shame as a "monument" within the subject's psyche created under the regimes of social and cultural rules and regulations, and that desire produces in the fetishist the rules of specific practices of the masochistic fantasy narrative he creates to bring amorphous shame under a formal control through a play of objects. In the nineteenth-century world, just as in contemporary times, the condition of radical social and cultural change—especially as concerns the body, sex, and gender—created the flourishing of incitements and practices that tend to "speak around" the issue but also infer a center of the discourse in retrospect. It is to these incitements and practices that subjects must attend, to secure the fortress against the increased blurring of these boundaries. Slippages in gender and sexual definitions in particular confound the subject's attempt to make meaning when the subject cannot resolve or dissolve the ambiguities and contradictions within. Individual subjects create practices to secure and stabilize social contradictions and ambiguities, and hence a strategy of securing the body and body image through costume play emerges as a bandage that covers the gaping ruptures. As Kaplan suggests, "[T]he primary aim of the fetishism strategy is to tame and subdue those human vitalities, which otherwise might overrun and destroy the universe."[21]

Fundamental to all contemporary social notions of "fetish" is the corset of the dominatrix, arguably one of the first items of clothing to be fetishized and easily the most important of fetish fashions.[22] While other manifestations of fetish wear remained hidden in the naughty backroom magazines of the twentieth century, the corset in various manifestations continued to play a subtle and sometimes surprising part in Western culture. Women's underwear adapted the corset into various versions of the garment: girdles, garter belts, teddies, and the playful but a bit naughty merry widow.[23] Frequently cited as part of the bride's trousseau (a now outmoded notion of fancy, sexy underwear to set the virginal bride up for her "opening night" performance in married life), these sorts of garments in the postmodern period have seen a resurgence in the now openly provocative wares of Victoria's Secret and Frederick's of Hollywood, among others.

A more transgressive though paradoxically overlooked manifestation can be seen on the costumes of American male comic book superheroes, from their inception in the mid-twentieth century to their contemporary forms. A particularly provocative example is *Spawn* (published by Image Comics and created by writer/artist Todd McFarlane, 1992 to the present).[24] In *Spawn*, the superhero (whose own troubled identity and manhood are the subjects of the initial narrative) sports the merry widow formation inscribed on his skinsuit: a red merry widow form trimmed in gray lines over a blue-black shiny skin. A break opens from between the breasts to the crotch below, inscribing a smooth *V* shape, more reminiscent of female genitalia than the usual bulge of male genitalia. Although Spawn behaves with machismo, the reader is privy to the inner doubts he has of his manhood, rendering ambivalent hints in his costume readable. Though this inscription seems to be more directly represented in postmodern superheroes such as Spawn, nevertheless, superheroes have been wearing a less overt version—the skinsuit, a constrictive garment discussed later—since their beginnings with *Superman* (1938–present).

Regardless of their application to character, the torso corset (like the lesser-known neck or penis corsets) constrict by tightening with a tube-like covering secured by a back-laced opening that is tied off in a bow. In its tightened form, it constricts the body to a point of pressure that results in pain or almost pain, difficulty in breathing, and the breasts and genital areas squeezed out to protuberance, with increased blood flow in those areas causing sexual excitement. From outside the body, the view creates variations according to current fashions of an hourglass figure: breasts are propelled upward into a highly visible profile, hips blossom out beyond the fictionalized narrows of the tiny waist. Contemporary designers of corsets, which have radically increased in number and visibility since the inception of the Internet, have used the corset not only to create works in many fabrics and media, but also to add elements that create a broader set of fantasy narratives than that of the nineteenth-century dominatrix. Also, corsets have branched out from strictly fetish to couture fashion, and they have called up a pastiche of fashion forms and practices, the most prominent being the Lolita and steampunk fashions of those subcultural communities. And although there are now wide and varied designs being created for the fetish community, a few emerge as examples of how fetish costumes have moved into fetish fashions, many of which are rapidly expanding into mainstream usage and copied by couturiers and independent designers.

The traditional dominatrix corset is the central and defining part of the dominatrix costume and performance. The historical image of the "French mistress," Steele postulates, illustrated by the letters of English schoolgirls as "fulfilling an important fantasy role," may have initiated the dominatrix image of the disciplinary female character. She suggests that "English people might have fantasized about the Continent at a time when French kisses, French letters, and French dresses had a special cachet."[25] This category of fetish fashion takes the French mistress in two directions—both involving constriction but also accentuating the "character" that becomes part of an appealing narrative. One is the dominatrix, usually in black leather or vinyl with heavy and tight lacings in the back, and generally refers to one of the many dominatrix character roles. Current fetish designers such as Dark Garden, Demask, Marquis, AMF, and Torture Garden Designs create many variations on the classic black dominatrix corset—both under-the-bust and over-the-bust models—as well as creative and technologically innovative alternatives. More dramatic versions exist, too: for instance, "Bondage Slut" (found on the *House of Harlot* website) features Eva Vortex, a famous transsexual and fetish icon, with other parts of the body also corseted, leaving only small areas of the body peeking through (see Figure 4.1). Her corset extends with straps over the enormous and rather magnificent breasts and joins with a neck corset that constrains head movement. The arms and legs—beginning under the crotch—are also corseted, although the leg corsets in this instance are referred to as "stockings," which can also be constricting elements. In this case, as happens frequently when the corset is constructed of heavy-gauge latex or rubber, the color is bright with details in contrasting colors to accentuate the lines that are so compelling for the wearer and the observer. The wearer is constricted but not without movement; she is able to move in such a way as to showcase her pressure-enhanced breasts and genital area, which serve to heighten and accentuate erotic sensations.

Fig. 4.1 The remarkable Eva Vortex demonstrates the variability of style in the costume of the Dominatrix. Photo courtesy of Eva Vortex.

Along with the expansion of technology and materials has come the expansion of corset forms and expressions that, though they still operate in the realm of fetish performance, in some cases have become works of extraordinary art. Louis Fleischauer's AMF Korsets are some of the most magical and stunning fetish objects in this category. All of his corsets are handmade, and in his work is also his fetish:

> I love slicing and stitching the leather its like caressing your lovers skin with the kiss of a blade. To open your lovers skin is the purest combination of love, lust and trust, the essence of this moment is what I want to externalize with the wounds I use to decorate my wearable art. Each piece reflects a different mood, a different desire. Sometimes the skin is clean and innocent, sometimes dirty, sliced and hold *[sic]* together by stitches . . . designed to invoke your deepest desires, you're covered in skin and the refection of your primal hunger. Inside the New Flesh you're more naked then *[sic]* before.[26]

The language of fetish is unmistakable: the lovingly concise and detailed description of his treatment of the leather or "skin" and the elevation of the act to that of art and love. And his work is indeed art. He has used the goal of constriction to create corset-based costumes that clearly evoke the fetish performance but are expanded to fantasy and dramatic narrative. Some have wings attached with a gothic satanic gloss; others have wings that are reminiscent of eroticized fairy-tale characters. Other corsets are embedded in an elaborate apparatus for suspension, which can pierce the skin of the S/M performer, adding the blood of the performer to the complexity of the corset's ornamentation and allure. He creates a complex, dark narrative basis for each collection—just as the couturiers do—and when shown in performance, they enact the fetish fairy tale in a rich variety of S/M motifs.

There is a level of constriction in this style that reverses the power valence from dominant to submissive, yet it retains the dark, mysterious power of the dominatrix as it reverberates in this most restrictive and transgressive fashion. Many fashions are versions of this theme, suggesting all the qualities of the dominatrix but swiveling the power quotient for a dramatic effect. The enclosed body corset and hood created by Jeroen van der van der Klis for Bizarre Fashion constricts all functions of the body by using a corset that extends its full length, from the hooded head and partial face through the neck and torso to the ankles. Arms and feet are also tightly corseted in laced boots and detached arm corsets. The fashion further constrains with straps that restrict the head from moving side to side by their secured position on the front and back of the shoulders. The body is held in place through strong straps attached to ceiling supports at the top of the hood, which forces the subject to stand faltering,

Fig. 4.2 Models Ophelia Overdose and Sinteque reveal the extraordinary beauty and range of the fantasy corset designs of Louis Fleischauer. Photo courtesy of Louis Fleischauer and AMF Corsets.

in a pivoting, tentative position on her toes. All control of the body is constricted and restricted by the dominant, leaving the submissive in a blinded delicate balance. Molded into the smooth, black leather penile shape by the corsets, she becomes the virtual "phallic woman," but this stands in deep paradox and irony through her utter lack of power or control; the stark aesthetic is compelling and beautiful, further inculcating the viewer into a subversive and submissive collaboration with the will of the dominant.

Fig. 4.3 Submissive Corset: hanging precariously from the top of the head mask, this submissive leather costume encloses and secures the entire body in a full-body corset, with stability only attained on the tips of the wearer's toes. This is the beautifully crafted work of Jeroen van der Klis of Bizarre Design at www.BizarreDesign.nl. Photo courtesy of Jeroen van der Klis.

With the entire body enclosed and squeezed, the skinsuit or *zentai* suit is implied. The *zentai* suit began as a costume allowing ballet, circus, and acrobatic performers to move freely and to exhibit the body in performance. Much later it became the basis for dance and sports costumes such as swimming suits and skiing costumes for similar reasons: ease of movement in activity and the exposure of the body. Lycra was invented in 1958, and vinyl, although created in the 1920s, through continual innovations was developed to a form that could be used as a fabric by the 1950s and 1960s.[27] But the improving qualities of rubber and "heavy rubber" have meant that the fulfilling sensations of constrictive bodysuits enjoyed by fetishists can be molded into fashions in an array of colors, with applications of ornamental aspects that not only represent characters but exponentially advance the tightening potential of the bodysuit. Rubber, Lycra, latex, and vinyl are used for corsets, gloves, stockings, hoods, masks, and boots for fetish fashions. But with these innovations in materials, fetish fashion began to move beyond the mere bodysuit for practitioners into remarkable and creative collections based on the bodysuit but expanding the potential for sexual fantasies.

Fetish fashion designers such as Marquis not only expanded their skinsuit fashions into an array of character types but also have moved into fashion design for the fetishist seeking constriction. For example, the rubber "Domina Dress Abbess" from Marquis is a combination of a dominatrix robe, with the "ends of the sleeves, hem and cleavage . . . framed with thick rubber tubing, and . . . openings over behind and crotch,"[28] and a top and catsuit bottom in transparent red rubber. Reminiscent of the 1960s work of André Courrèges, both in form and color, the Domina dress reveals the potential for erotic skinsuits to emerge into fashion that—if not quite so revealing— might appear on a mainstream runway.

Rubber and spandex skinsuits are also used in the composition of character suits such as nurse, maid, and military costumes, as well as the many dominatrix characters. As a base for costume, the skinsuit provides a highly constricted, shiny, colorful, and (most importantly) clearly artificial effect for the body of the wearer. The ornamentation that signifies the essential aspects of that character for the fetishist is caricatured and accentuated with an intriguing humorous and childlike effect. They resemble the Halloween costumes for children in their bold shapes and naive signs, but juxtaposed with the overt shiny sexuality of the compressed and eroticized body image the skinsuit projects, the combined result is one of a sort of condescension—a perfect nuance for the dominatrix and her submissive. These are the costumes that dominate the websites of Torture Garden and its gallery of fetish designers, as well as many of the other fetish design sites.

Beyond the realm of skinsuit fetish fashions ready for prime time are the deeper, more subversive desires for suffocation as part of the extreme effect of constriction. This is a particular sector of the constriction fetishists who respond to the danger of suffocation, strangulation, and potentially death. There are several ways in which variations of the skinsuit are manipulated into costume forms to deliver this sensation. Marquis Bazaar Bizarre, the online store for fetish wear by Marquis, offers several options: the most benign seems to be the "Latex Amniotic Sac," essentially

Fig. 4.4 This "Domina" vinyl fashion found on the Marquis web-site constricts but also is very fashionable, reminiscent of the work of André Courrèges in his use of geometrics and PVC in the 1960s. Photo courtesy of Peter W. Czernich.

a latex bag into which the fetishist can climb into (and supposedly climb out of), which forces the body into a fetal-like position, reviving the prenatal sensation of security and confinement. The "Bodybag Stretchy" is a bodysuit that encases the torso, coming together at the crotch to form "shorts," and is entered from the back of the costume, giving the wearer "sufficient room to fondle yourself, but . . . unable to fend off manipulations from outside."[29]

Deeper into the constrictive body bag potential is Marquis's "Bodybag Extrem." Apparently "long awaited," this is a full body bag of heavy transparent grey rubber that extends from the attached helmet to over the feet and face. There is one hole for breathing, but otherwise, the fetishist is completely covered in this long, tight bag that secures the fetishist in a rigid standing or prone position—hands tightly glued to the sides of the body, legs and feet bound together—negating any possibility of movement. But there is also the "Body Bag," which is a black or transparent zip-up latex bag for multiple partners, which is "extremely flexible" and "big enough for everybody."[30] Finally, Marquis offers a "Rubber Vacuum Bed," for which details are not offered, but the image is of a figure frozen in position under a vacuum-sealed surface of black rubber.

Character

A rather remarkable example of the fetish skinsuit is demonstrated by Mistress Jean Bardot in her famous skinsuit sporting outrageously outsize breasts and vagina. This is not just for constriction but is a fetish costume created to perform and to be viewed as a comical yet still seductive fetishized feminine identity. Her performance in this suit parades a dominating female persona through the dominating presence of the female body. Thus, the suit acts as a constrictive costume as well as a flagrant sign of feminine dominance and character.

Fig. 4.5 Mistress Jean Bardot, known for her humor and sensuality, poses in a skinsuit designed to both amuse and seduce. Photo courtesy of Gil Perron.

Character is linked to identity in subtle but compelling ways. *Identity* is an extremely difficult and highly contested term, but in general, identity represents "the collective aspect of the set of characteristics by which a thing is definitively recognizable or known . . . [and further], the set of characteristics by which an individual is recognizable."[31] In his extensive examination of the "problem of the construction of the 'self,'" Foucault suggests that, "The self may be theorized in terms of the conceptual and other intellectual resources that it calls upon in order to write or talk about itself, and in the way in which it is written about, or written to."[32] In other words, identity is a construct of both the interior comprehension and recognition of the self by the subject as well as those "signs" that evoke recognition by the social and cultural exterior. The interior construct, according to many cultural theories, is created from the way the subject has been "called out" or addressed by family, friends, schools, media, and other cultural institutions as a particular type of subject. These addresses are essential and elemental, calling the subject out in terms of gender, race, sexuality, class, and any other way in which we recognize ourselves or are recognized by those outside ourselves: *all* understandings of identity are mediated by these aspects of consciousness and social relations. This is essentially the theory of "Interpellation" developed by Louis Althusser, wherein the societal and cultural institutions—which Althusser referred to as ISAs (ideological state apparatus)—create the subject's identity, "opposing Marx's contention that humans were the authors of their own destiny with the view that social relations are instrumental in the construction of identity, belief systems and forms of consciousness."[33] As a patchwork of a lifetime of mediated identifications, then, the identity of the subject would seem to be under the subject's control, but few are detached enough to perceive this recognition or strong enough to accept those controls. Yet there is one way through which individuals, including fetishists, have actualized this sort of control throughout history: through performance of characters in a fictional narrative or ritual.

The definition of *character* runs very close to the dictionary definition of *identity*, as *character* is defined as "The qualities that distinguish one person from another . . . a person portrayed in a drama or novel."[34] It is close in its description of the "qualities that distinguish" to identity's "set of characteristics by which a thing is definitively recognizable or known," in that both address certain aspects or qualities that set individuals apart in terms of elements that are visible from both inside and outside the subject. Yet the added description of character as a person "portrayed in a drama" insinuates the suggestion of a "portrayal" of a person, or an act of *substitution* of one set of characteristics that are allied with the identity of the subject for another set of characteristics that are part of a character's fictional identity within a narrative in performance. This notion of the substitution in human expression reminds us also of the ways in which fetish has been described and defined. Is there a link? Garber recites a description by Freud in which Garber is then able to link these notions:

Freud writes about the fetish that it replaces the imagined maternal phallus: "Something else has taken its place, has been appointed its substitute, as it were, and now inherits the interest which was formerly directed to its predecessor . . . What other men have to woo and make exertions for can be had by the fetishist with no trouble at all." But this mechanism of substitution, which is the trigger of transvestite fetishism, is also the very essence of theater: role-playing, improvisation, costume, and disguise . . . [that is], something fundamental about the way dramatic representation works—and about the power of the transvestite.[35]

This linkage of identities, characters, fetishes, costumes, and theater secures the method by which certain fetishists (drag queens and kings and other transvestites) are able to be visible in the mainstream—albeit as Others—but it also secures the method by which fetishes and fetish performances work to achieve an erotic and spiritual climax. In addition, we can also enlist the various practices and predilections of fetish in the world of high fashion, highly insinuated by its fantasies, its runway shows, and its models and their poses. As a result, there are primarily character-type costumes portrayed on fetish designer websites and publications. Made with constricting materials, these costumes perform double-duty in fulfilling fetish desires. Yet most of the costumes are found for the performance of the central character in fetish performances.

The primary character role in fetish play, as a result of its singular association with the maternal phallic power, is of course the dominatrix, the "mother" to a wide range of fetish narratives and desires. The roles of the dominatrix—the nurse, the maid, the lion tamer, the cat woman, military captain, the governess, the prostitute—all extend from the founding image of the domineering Victorian French mistress. Worn here (Figure 4.6) by Mistress Jean Bardot, this costume is but one of the many variations possible of the style. Her Victorian "gown" is constructed of shiny black inflated rubber balloons, a shiny black vinyl corset bodice laced both above and below the bared breasts, accessorized by high-heeled black "fetish" shoes and a nasty little whip; Mistress Jean condescends to address the viewer of the photograph. Her erect stance, her delicate fingering of the whip, and her pert miniaturized version of the male top hat (a key symbol of the *habit noir*) sitting in a cocky position on her head as she looks down at the viewer are all very carefully constructed signs of her dominance and part of a highly detailed costume of the dominatrix fashion. Extraordinarily provocative, her nudity, the active symbology of her costume, and her "acting" of the character of the punishing Victorian French mistress both invite and disdain the viewer. She is both beautiful and terrible, both masculine and feminine, both real and imaginary, both serious and ironically comic. For the fetishist in particular, she represents a panoply of cultural and costume signs that are as subversive in contemporary culture as they were in the nineteenth century. Garber suggests that in the nineteenth century, "[a]ctors were in effect *allowed* to violate the sumptuary laws that governed dress and social station—on the supposedly 'safe' area of the stage . . . a privileged site of transgression, in which *two* kinds of transvestism were permitted to players: changes of costume that violated edicts against wearing the wrong rank as well as the wrong gender."[36]

Fig. 4.6 Mistress Jean Bardot in her costume reminiscent of rococo excesses and "overblown" style—designed for grand entrances. Photo courtesy of Drayke Larson of Photosynthetique.

Mistress Jean in her contemporary version of the dominatrix costume demonstrates the same dichotomy between accepted dress and class, albeit through contemporary sumptuary and class rules. In the role of the dominating female, she represents the very essence of the gender troubles of the late twentieth and early twenty-first centuries: she is masculine in her overwhelming powerful and disdainful persona but feminine in her overt erotic display of a female body. Cast in shiny black rubber, she emulates the highly fetishized S/M costumes of the mid-twentieth century motorcycle subculture, typified by images of the deeply marginalized homosexual male icons of artist Tom of Finland. Representing class not as a social ranking of wealth and race but as a gender role, and specifically as the highly guarded (necessarily so at the time) elitism of the gay underworld of the Leathermen, Mistress Jean has transgressed into the most profoundly, deeply male of all male cultural institutions. As Steele explains,

> According to British fashion writer Colin McDowell, the origin of leather's appeal lies in the fact that "the unaroused penis [is] pink and pathetic." Leather provides a reassuring symbol of virile male sexuality. Not only does a leather jacket "disguise" the body's "inadequacies" and provide a sense of "heightened sexual awareness," but it also functions as an icon of butch, raunchy, even brutal, masculinity—and raw power . . . Symbolically, leather is equated with pain, power, "animalistic and predatory impulses"—and masculinity.[37]

Fig. 4.7 Mistress Jean Bardot is prepared to punish in the traditional dominatrix gear. Photo courtesy of Drayke Larson of Photosynthetique.

Thus is the transgression of the dominatrix deeply embedded—and somewhat hidden—in a costume that dares to juxtapose the extreme "girly" Victorian fashions with the hard, brutal sexuality and extreme exclusivity of the dominant gay male, feminizing the most sacred power of the most underground of male cultures. Garber cites this as a "category crisis," in which there is a "failure of definitional distinction, a borderline that becomes permeable, that permits border crossings," but Mistress Jean, in her lack of clear definitional distinction and as a compendium of transvestitic signs, becomes a "space of possibility structuring and confounding culture: the disruptive element that intervenes, not just a category crisis of male and female, but the crisis of category itself."[38]

From this point, the dominatrix moves on to new roles invented by the dominatrix and the "submissives" themselves. Many of these character roles are based in the nurturing and caretaking roles of women for children (the governess), the sick (the nurse), the sinner (the nun), the subordinate (the military captain), the master or mistress (the maid), the serf (the countess), the pet (the lion tamer, owner), the baby (the babysitter), and more.

In using the uniform and "duties" of the greatly revised and sexualized versions of these roles, a titillation is created that vibrates in a gap created through the ironic paradoxes that exist between the swiveling contradictions of the maid as both dominant and submissive. This upholds the various master/slave theories acknowledged by McClintock in her description of an

> [o]rganized subculture shaped around the ritual exercise of social risk and social transformation. As a theater of conversion, S/M reverses and transforms the social meanings it borrows . . . S/M is a theater of transformation; it "plays the world backward" . . . visibly and outrageously staging hierarchy, difference and power, the irrational ecstasy, or alienation of the body . . . hence the paradox of S/M. On the one hand, S/M parades a slavish obedience to conventions of power . . . At the same time, with its exaggerated emphasis on costumery, script and scene, S/M reveals that social order is unnatural, scripted and invented.[39]

Thus the gap is distinguished as the location of climactic transformation: the moment in which the powerless is also simultaneously all-powerful.

This particular "theatrical trick" can also be seen actively in the character of the nurse, performed here (Figure 4.8) by Mistress Jean Bardot. As with all of the character designs, there are numerous versions and variations, but they all seem to deliver the same significations and implications for sexual desire. As nurse, she wears a parody of the uniform constructed of rubber. The tight fit of the dress acts as a constrictive apparatus; and the sign of the nurse is indicated through the white cross emblazoned on the nurse's hat. Accompanied by a submissive "patient" in a zentai suit ready and waiting for treatment in the chair. Mistress Jean glowers invitingly down at the viewer with swept-back hair and minimal make-up, but the focus is on her gloves. Gloves—now playing a part in a greater variety of character roles through the improvements made in the malleability of latex, vinyl, and rubber—can give the fetish character special effects: for instance, masquerading

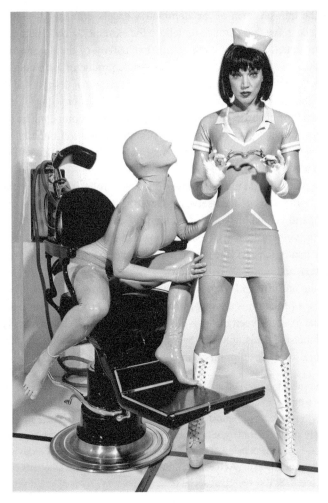

Fig. 4.8 Mistress Jean Bardot acts as a "nurse" ready to subject her client to medical interventions. Photo courtesy of Gil Perron.

as webbed, hoofed, or amputated-stump limbs. Wearing medical latex gloves, Mistress Jean uses these signs of her power in the carefully constructed gestures of her hands as, in her capable hands, she holds an instrument of "intervention" in an insinuation of genital penetration, and gestures toward the viewer of this photograph in an invitation to join the action. The gloves are stretched-out tool to accentuate its constrictive and painful potential. This "act" construes once again the paradoxical character of this usually helpful female role: this nurse accentuates her intent to create pain, not alleviate it. But she also carries the potential for sexual excitation and climax with her overt implication of sadomasochistic "operations" to be fulfilled.

In one of the most compelling and provocative roles of the dominatrix, Mistress Jean takes on the role of the *flâneur* of the late nineteenth century. The costume of the *flâneur*, or dandy, is described by Lehmann as "(Morning) coat, trousers, and . . . the *gilet*, all cut from one piece of fabric, [which] stood for . . . a new sobriety expressed by an almost invariable costume . . . that paraphrased the new bourgeois virtues of decency and frugality."[40] And indeed, as she is posed in the profile of the master, Mistress Jean's black rubber skinsuit is inscribed with subtle diagonals that suggest the gilet (or waistcoat) juxtaposed with the vertical stripes that indicate the topcoat (or surtout) and trousers of the *habit noir*. In her tightly gloved hands, ready to strike, is a horsewhip, a trace of the *habit noir*'s origins in the male riding costume of the late eighteenth century but also a weapon in S/M's arsenal of pleasurable punishments. Atop her head is a bowler hat, an interesting alternative to the dandy's black top hat, which had acted as a ubiquitous sign of the late nineteenth century masculinity and "bourgeois society, its morality and aspirations . . . [and] by the first decade of the twentieth century . . . already appeared dated and reminiscent of a more sophisticated age."[41] The bowler hat was invented in 1849 by the London hatmakers Thomas and William Bowler, who were commissioned by a customer to design a close-fitting, low-crowned hat to protect his gamekeepers' heads, since the top hat was continually knocked off by low-hanging branches while they were on horseback.[42] At the time, the bowler was considered an informal hat for daily wear and at times was associated with the working class and the sporting world, hence its alternate title of "derby" (as in the Kentucky Derby) and its place in the iconology of the working-class artist René Magritte. But when the bowler continued in use as the top hat faded in the early twentieth century, it became associated in popular culture with the traditional British gentleman (again, we can use John Steed from *The Avengers* (1961–1969) as a typical example).

Mistress Jean's modernist *flâneur* costume, then, is loaded with nuance and innuendo, as most fetish costumes are. The contradictions and paradoxical significations add to the piquancy of her performance as the implications of class, gender, and even species collide in the gaps created from this parodic performance. Mistress Jean is cleverly utilizing the "gamekeeper" identity of this *habit noir*, as indicated by her bowler hat and horsewhip. She is therefore dominating over livestock, indicating the submissive as domesticated animal and perhaps—to the great satisfaction and titillation of the S/M submissive—the lowest level of animal identity. She is posed in a modernist masculine stance of power and authority, her whip in the ready position and her smile indicating her pleasure at the potential for action. Yet through the beauty and grace of her bodily profile, now shining in black rubber, her femininity is also and at the same time present, once again placing the strict modernist values and gender roles into a performance of threatening ambiguity and paradox. Particularly in this postmodern era wherein Mistress Jean is performing, modernism itself is also in play: she is juxtaposing modernism, whose authoritarian and patriarchal values and commodities still exist in the overlap of the colliding cultures, with the

Fig. 4.9 Mistress Jean Bardot cross-dresses as the *flâneur*. Photo courtesy of Gil Perron.

postmodern multiplicity of gendered identities that are fragmenting the masculine edifice of authority into a plethora of hybridized gender citations and identities. This gap now filled with the charged particles of difference, "the congruences and diversities hidden within the social fabric become apparent in textiles and accessories. Observing them, the historian is able to realize the 'revolutionary potential' in a more direct manner, while the artist can employ them as metaphors for another reality."[43]

A deeper level of subversion and difference from mainstream culture in the assumption of character fashions can be found in the much-misunderstood paraphilic infantilist.[44] Paraphilic infantilism is a defined by the desire to wear diapers, for reasons other than medical requirement, and/or to be cared for as a baby or toddler. Within their community, those adults who desire only the titillation or intimacy of diaper changing without desiring the fantasy of babyhood, are called "Diaper Lovers" (or DLs).[45] If the DL is also interested in punishment role-playing— a smaller subset of this fetish—they are referred to as "S/M/DLs."[46] In terms of fetish fashion, these fetishists frequently wear adult diapers under their usual everyday clothes. The adult who is only interested in the infantilistic play and intimacy is called an Adult Baby (or AB). Adults who desire all aspects are referred to as AB/DLs. In 2004, a casual cyberspace survey of eighty fully grown diaper wearers revealed approximately forty percent believed themselves to be purely DLs, about forty percent of respondents were mixed, and twenty percent of respondents believed themselves purely ABs.[47] The study also suggested that a substantial number of respondents were adolescents engaged in this practice. Findings of the American Psychiatric Association propose that the bulk of infantilists are heterosexual men.[48] However, at a social event for the "Still in Diapers NY" group (SIDNY) in 2002, half of the participants identified as homosexual men, and a growing number are women.[49] Yet importantly, none of the respondents are sexually attracted to children; as my source, Baby Dani,[50] stated, rather than be attracted to children, they identify themselves with children. Sexual attraction is with the "mother," the caretaker, or "babysitter," who takes care of their needs, both physical and emotional.

A 1988 survey created by Dr. Thomas Sargent suggests who the average infantilist is:

> A male, who has a bachelors or higher degree, in a management position, and is a heterosexual. He was usually the youngest child in a family. His parents were not divorced, or dead, and he was raised by both parents. He was not physically or mentally abused as a child, and feels he was treated normally for his age while growing up. Half were bed wetters when children. He can have a sexual relationship in or out of diapers, but prefers to wear them as a sexual "turn-on."[51]

With some key differences, this description follows my interviewee, Baby Dani.[52] Baby Dani represents another offshoot of the infantilists, the "sissy baby," or crossdressing AB or AB/DL, which might involve "stereotypical or exaggerated 'little girl' clothing, such as frilly panties or dresses. Sissies are not necessarily transsexual in that while some might be expressing an alter ego that is a baby girl, they might not wish to be an adult woman at other times."[53]

When I first saw Baby Dani, she was watching the performance at Ground Zero[54] of Mistress Jean Bardot's fetish theater. I was struck by the high level of craft and design of her costume: her pink plaid pleated skirt was beautifully wrought and topped with a pink fuzzy hoodie, with pink ribbons, immaculate white tights, and Mary Jane shoes. I met with her and discovered that she is, in her everyday life, an attractive

Fig. 4.10 Shy "Baby Dani" is an Adult Baby whose sweet baby girl fashions drew my attention to her. Photo courtesy of Drayke Larson of Photosynthetique.

businessman in his late thirties or early forties, tall and fit. He was divorced with children—none of his family knows about his "other life"—and he currently dated women and looked forward to meeting someone who would not only understand his need but be willing to, at least on some level, participate in his life. Charming, open, and articulate, he explained his origins in his need to find a community, and by accident, he had arrived at Ground Zero for the fetish performance. The level of acceptance and community for what was an audience of radically different fetishists profoundly moved him. He began to consider himself and his own desires and realized that he would fit in the category of a sissy baby. As an infant, he had been an orphan, and when he was adopted by a family, his older sisters babied him, which was his first experience in love and physical attention. He displayed no sense of shame discussing his identification but rather a cheery wistfulness that he had attempted to integrate his lives together. He educated me on the AB and DL categories and his attitude and difficulty in getting baby clothes in his size. The cost and complications of Internet ordering make getting clothes difficult, expensive, and time-consuming.

An online search found few designers who posted openly; instead, discreet sites and E-bay postings from individual seamstresses seem to be the only sources available. The costumes seemed to be designed primarily as copies of existing children's clothing, frequently advertised with the image of an actual infant in the garment or, increasingly, with the adult costume modeled by attractive young women, such as found on privatina.eu.[55] It is as if the image of the primary user, an adult male, is too transgressive even on a site devoted to precisely these users. Baby Dani must depend on clothing makers he finds online and through the community. Even a Lolita designer told me that she shied away from designing costumes for the fetish community, but she was reluctant to explain why. The taboo of males in infant girls' costumes perhaps garners the most disgust, given that the cultural image of males on any level of society is still at the top of the gender power scale, and the infant girl is at the bottom as the most helpless, most vulnerable, yet the most appealing. Fernbach explains this phenomenon through her concept of "decadent fetishism":

> Decadent fetishism can be transgressive of hegemonic hierarchized binaries, either by inverting the binary, or by celebrating non-hierarchized difference. Rather than disavowing difference by making the Other the Same, decadent fetishism tends to proliferate differences. Decadent fetishism involves an identification with the Other and a fantasy of self-transformation that offers a critique, in a fashion, of hegemonic hierarchized binaries.[56]

This "critique of hegemonic binaries" in a culture thick with radical change toward power structures and gender roles—such as the late nineteenth, late twentieth, and early twenty-first centuries—has been made manifest through the visible marks and signs of fashion. The infantilists, who must traverse the most profound and dangerous of liminal boundaries, consequently must mine their fashions from the most covert sources and perform their identity in small private venues and community parties, such as the SIDNY group. The images of such parties that do make it to the Internet become instant objects of mockery and cruel commentary. On the *Huffington Post*'s "Huffpost Style" section, after a description of a pair of adult ruffled panties sold at Forever 21, Rachel Kane remarks, "Merry Christmas, pervs."[57] Yet the community longs for fashions—not just clothes—and as society traverses its long path toward acceptance of all genders and sexualities, perhaps the infantilist will gain its fashion designers.

Effectuation

Finally, *effectuation*, which refers to a bringing about of a certain effect,[58] characterizes a class of fetish costume and performance that are used directly on or in the subject's body for sexual gratification. This includes a wide variety of designs of gloves, shoes, boots, whips, bondage straps and gear, gags, and masks with various peculiar accoutrements for actions on or to the subject. This is the most subversive and, frankly, the most disturbing category for most "vanilla" non-fetishists. It garners the most fear and sexual disgust because of a sense of dehumanization and degradation for the subject using—or "being used by"—these costumes.

Yet it is usually part of the S/M fetish performance and of fetish fashion and accessories. Under the modernist regime, the male is so utterly the strong authoritarian, the ideal gender, the proud example of our species. Because of this, when we see the male submissive—despite many essays to the contrary, the overwhelming predominant gender in this role—not only enduring but reveling in sexually explicit acts of degradation meted out by a dominant female, we respond with complete disgust and abjection. Yet this degradation is precisely what the submissive seeks. The part abjection plays has been much discussed by feminist philosophers and critics in this way:

Fig. 4.11 "Baby Dani" has been naughty, it seems, and Mistress Jean metes out her punishment. Photo courtesy of Drayke Larson of Photosynthetique.

Abjection, as Julia Kristeva puts it, "draws me toward the place where meaning collapses" . . . At the same time as threatening the current symbolic order, abjection provides the opportunity for its reworking, precisely insofar as it represents a crisis in meaning. By paying attention to abject moments, and to moments that produce and follow them, moments in which identity appears to coagulate and cover over the fissures and cracks that help to produce it, we can contest the forces that tend to gain hegemonic power over us.[59]

This is to say, by submerging himself in degrading sexual positions, the male fetishist subverts and "calls out" the very cultural confines that produced the impossible ideal he struggles and necessarily always fails to emulate. Furthermore, by paying attention to the proliferation of such behavior in males, the problem of the deeply embedded and naturalized conception of prescribed gender roles is brought forward into the discourse. As McClintock and other critics acknowledge, this sort of phenomenon is always present but increases exponentially in times of cultural crises. Many critics suggest that in creating groups—such as fetish clubs and private parties—these extremely marginalized subjects create, through the recognition of a collective acceptance of different realms of desire, a form of collective agency. This power forms riffs in the fabric of mainstream culture, and its disdain and abjection of these subjects and their acts—which is also recognition—causes the discourse around gender roles to be challenged or, at the very least, questioned.

Objects of Effectuation

Gloves are one of the most ubiquitous symbols of sexual performance and entirely indicative of the sexual connotations of sexuality and genital forms. While the fingers protrude into phallic forms, the wearer of the glove also feminizes the glove as fingers are inserted into the narrow vaginal shapes. The image of the empty glove lying about, the dropped glove, the delicate positioning of gloved hands with fingers drawn out or curled like petals in a provocatively beckoning gesture all attest to the power of the glove to symbolize the role they most often perform: as a seductive phallic substitute to be sucked, caressed, or stroked. To further its allure, the tight glove provides the pleasure of constriction, but it most often plays a key part in a series of S/M narratives and rituals and, not surprisingly, in historical courting rituals:

> There were . . . references to "punishment gloves" that could be locked . . . "Covering the organs of touch . . . gloves . . . emphasize sexual insinuations by simultaneously reining in and stimulating desire" . . . while pornography associates the hand with masturbation (hence the old expression "hand job"). In the Middle Ages, references to scented gloves evoked female genitals, and gloves were exchanged between lovers.[60]

Gloves also play a key role in the character aspect of fetish, particularly for the new "species" fetish groups such as the "Furries,"[61] where gloves can be paws, webbed feet, or hoofs, facilitating a four-footed fetish "fursona."

Fig. 4.12 Mistress Jean Bardot demonstrates one of the effectual uses of gloves. Photo of Drayke Larson of Photosynthetique.

Shoes also facilitate the role of the four-footed fursonas. Valerie Steele seems to suggest that shoe fetishism emerged in the eighteenth century,[62] citing as a particularly graphic example the French writer Restif de La Bretonne (1734–1806), who in his novel described how the narrator, in kissing one of his wife's shoes, ejaculated into the other.[63] I doubt she was amused. Nevertheless, shoes and particularly high-heeled shoes became associated with women and femininity by the modern period. High heels are associated with bondage, the precariousness of stability and therefore danger, and, for certain fetishists, the delightful potential for being stepped on with a needle-like heel.

But it also bore another of the shoe fetish's key attractions, the "dildo-like" shape of the toe of the shoe. Just as with a Viennese boot from the nineteenth century, whose heel was shaped for anal penetration,[64] the use of the shoe as an active phallic substitute positions the male shoe fetishist in the passive position, one who responds to the female shoe or boot as a symbol of phallic power, aggression, and perhaps even violence. The shoe or boot also tends to be a focus for another related fetish, that

Fig. 4.13 Mistress Jean Bardot shows off her phallic high heels. Photo courtesy of Drayke Larson of Photosynthetique.

of the male S/M slave. According to an interview with a male slave, his submissive position was associated with the act of kissing the boots of the dominant female—usually the dominatrix. Historically, the foot and therefore the shoe and boot, with its position as the lowest part of the body that treads on the dirt of the earth, has been fetishized as locus for power negotiations. Yet Steele points out that Ernest Becker draws a sharp distinction between foot and shoe:

> "The foot is its own horror; what is more, it is accompanied by its own striking and transcending denial and contrast—the shoe" . . . Whereas the foot is a low and dirty "testimonial to our degraded animality," the shoe—made of soft and shiny polished leather with an elegantly curved arch and pointed toe, lifted above ground on a hard spiked heel—"is the closest thing *to* the body and yet not *the* body."[65]

This is a compelling notion that may inform many of the fantasies of shoe fetishists, but as Steele also points out, for many foot/shoe/boot fetishists, it was both the foot and its coverings that delighted, and in a wide variety of conditions—from dirty, sweaty feet to delicate tiny "lotus" shapes, and from elegant leather spiked high-heeled shoes to tough, black motorcycle boots. There are even "toe cleavage" fetishists, who are titillated by the juncture between the big and second toe revealed in many women's high-heeled shoes, a miniature of the low-cut neckline. Steele suggests that the foot acts as a surrogate for the body parts that are exposed, and perhaps those that are not. Further, there are fetishists who fetishize the high-heeled shoe or boot for the effect it has on the body of the female, the intense flexion of calf muscles and the way it cants the female body forward, forcing breasts and buttocks outward and back arched to keep balance when walking. With this varied array of responses and desires centered on the foot/shoe/boot, it follows that "foot and shoe fetishism is widely believed to be the commonest type of fetishism."[66]

But perhaps the most subversive, debased, and possibly degrading effectual costume object is the mask. In fetish practice, the pleasure arises not just from the masking of the submissive identity but often from the added mechanisms of penetration and deposition from the body of the dominant toward the highly constricted, identity-less, faceless, orifice-less, and featureless head of the submissive. Yet masks in popular culture are paradoxically associated with torturers, burglars, and executioners—in short, the aggressor or deliverer of the punishment. In S/M and Leathersex, masks are used for both functions, emphasizing the pivoting positions of master/slave that swivel the power quotient in such a satisfactory way for the fetishist.

How do these fetish masks work? Once again, there is a flurry of paradoxes surrounding the functions and effects of the fetish mask. What masks conceal and what they reveal circulate around the performance of masquerade. The masquerade is a performance of the power relations in play in contemporary culture, manifested through social relations, gender roles, race, class, and sexual orientations. It "plays" society in a parodic masque of stereotyped characters using the props and costumes that represent the more nefarious objects and characters acting as "punctums"[67] in a particular image of society. Roland Barthes's notion of "punctums" identifies

> [a] detail or spot that arrests the viewer's eye, or as Barthes says, "pricks" it. Refusing conformity with any creative logic, the *punctum* is a point of real violence, which in its sheer contingency, oddity, or even uncanniness violates the familiar codes of [the visual elements, which are easily read because of the highly conventionalized codes of the culture]. The *punctum* challenges the viewer, who feels himself under scrutiny, challenged to make sense of what is seen.[68]

This is to say, the objects and subjects that present an uncanny or subversive presence in our "view" of culture become "pricks" (ah, how interestingly appropriate) of awareness that all is not acceptable, or understandable, or comprehensible in the culture. They stand out or "do violence" to our sensibilities apart from the vast panorama of accepted culture.

What does the mask conceal? It certainly attempts to conceal the subject's identity, though in reality most observers can identify the subject as a submissive, and, under the concept of identity, can recognize all the aspects that make up the founding identity—the psychological, the social, the sexual, the anxieties and satisfactions. But Henry Krips also suggests a "double deception"—a "deception that paradoxically depends upon the deceived seeing though another deception . . . [but] the one against whom the deception is practiced is the same one who deceives";[69] that is, the fetishist dons the mask to be annihilated, but not really. What is revealed is that he understands explicitly this is *theater*: that he is playing the role of the utterly submissive and that in reality it is *he*—not the masochistic slave he has *asked* and usually *paid* to play—who is directing the action, who is in fact the master. So what is being concealed are the actual power mechanisms of the fetish S/M performance, the master who has employed the dominatrix to play the master while he plays the submissive in order to fulfill his own psychosexual satisfaction.

Thanks to technical advances in rubber, the strongest referred to as "heavy rubber," any shape of fetish mask that is required by the fetishist can be manufactured, and indeed, websites such as Marquis[70] offer a number of options for the profoundly submissive subject. The level of submissive designs may shock the "vanilla" crowd, but it serves the fetish communities in their varied and multitudinous needs. And perhaps the "effect" extends to the level of mainstream shock: perhaps part of the *jouissance* comes from the distinct difference, and therefore a dark elitism, that comes from plumbing the depths of human sexuality that provides part of the titillation. As one Ground Zero regular suggested to me, "We are a tight underground group, and we like it like that."

Fetish Style: Fashion as Fetish

Changes in fashion reflect the dullness of nervous impulses; the more nervous the age, the more rapidly its fashions change, simply because the desire for differentiation, one of the most important elements of all fashion, goes hand in hand with the weakening of nervous energy.

Georg Simmel: "Fashion" in The Rise of Fashion[1]

Wherein Modernity "Jumps the Shark"

Tumbling out from the closets of long-repressed modern Western cultures came the postmodern outcasts: the gamers, cosplayers, anime otaku, skateboarders, Goths, punks, Lolitas, homosexuals, transsexuals, transvestites, tight-lacers, shoe-and-boot-kissers, human carpets, submissive slaves, dominatrices, Adult Babies, bondage worshippers, tattooed and surgically modified bodies, and a large contingent of yet-to-be-identified other fetishes, either too taboo to be part of the fetish performance or too mundane to mention. All of the aforesaid made their first public appearances as modes of fashion, with a costume or accessory, manipulated by emerging designers such as Vivienne Westwood to be shocking (but not repellent) and fun (but with meaning). Bucking the mainstream by voguing their way in through the club cultures, these designers and performers were found in key European and American cities and marked a radical change in the evolution of the fetish performance:

Molded by corsetry, tattooed, and pierced . . . marking the subject as existing outside of social norms and mainstream desires and identifying the body as a member of a loose-knit tribe or subculture . . . [these fetish performers] share a common definition of fetishism, one that is primarily concerned with the celebration of difference . . . fetishism no longer implies a situation where the fetishist needs a fetish in order for sexual arousal to take place. Instead, [they] speak of a type of fetishism where transformation of the body or self is paramount, and mainstream categories, including beliefs about gender, sexuality and the body, are transgressed . . . they directly oppose the meanings ascribed to psychoanalytic fetishism in contemporary theory.[2]

Its linkage with fashion and the fashion world is unmistakable; for example, to enter the KitKat Club in Berlin, you *must be dressed* in fetish.[3] And the play between the words *fashion* and *fetish* has begun to confound and complicate both their meanings and their designations. Fashion and fetish were, in modernity, separate concepts. However, postmodernity has meant a recognition of fashion as an obsessive behavior motivated by the hegemonic and eroticized meanings that circulate around the dressed or costumed body, as well as a societal power valance that has charged certain types and styles—particularly the couture fashion forms. These changes have propelled fashion into a primary theoretical consideration. No longer the domain of the frivolous female with too much money, fashion has exploded into a cornucopia of different uses, users, and venues made complex by the constellation of desires and practices that have pushed fashion into fetish categories.

Fetish is recognized no longer as the dark demimonde of perverts and prostitutes but as a "fashionable" evening, a titillating nuance, a high-fashion style. It is also noted in its quotidian use in the life of signs: the Christian cross, the national flag (particularly in sports and military), the T-shirt with cute quotations or popular copyrighted images, the new car design, the hot male and/or female pop star, the favorite pair of shoes; all are recognized as being fetishized by users without denigration, except perhaps with a slight moue of disdain. Fetish, though now very fashionable, is still associated with a certain weakness or slight abjection that is paradoxically part of its allure.

Ultimately, it cannot be denied that from any possible interpretation of the term *fetish*, indeed *fashion is fetish*. Fashion as an industry, a publication phenomenon, a collection of personas (the "fashionista," the model, the critics, the power players, the adoring society), and a highly influential force in contemporary culture that circulates around this splendored array of subjects, objects, and practices positions it as a fetishizing of clothing. Yet as Georg Simmel insists, "Fashion is always class-based,"[4] explaining,

> Fashion—i.e. the latest fashion—. . . affects only the upper classes. Social evolution . . . demands that as soon as the lower classes begin to adopt a particular fashion and thus destroy both the distinction between classes and the coherence of each respective class, the upper echelons discard their old clothes and put on new styles in order to retain differentiation—"thus the game goes merrily on."[5]

Of course, contemporary consumers understand this process much better than even Simmel's public may have: we all understand that a dress from a couture house can be priced at $3,000, and in a matter of a year or so, a similar design can be bought for a price in the double or even single digits off the sale rack at H&M—a shoddily made copy, wrinkled with threads still hanging, looking like a dried-up bouquet, yet because of its passing resemblance to the couture model, it is still desirable and now available to all classes. As the time frame for this process gets shorter and shorter, and consumers are ever-pressed by slowing economics, the gap between the couture dress and the dreadful copy become acceptable to even bourgeois consumers, looking for style but not willing or perhaps able to pay the price. Currently, the middle-ground designs that used to provide a reasonable copy at a reasonable price, though not quite as elegant, are quickly diminishing as the classes under the conservative culture polarize the class system into two options: upper and lower classes.

Yet—and here is a further paradox—the fetish fashions that have influenced couture fashions since the late 1990s have been historically located at the lowest class levels: they are the costumes of "perverts and prostitutes." In a clash of classes, fetish enters the couture fashion scene not from the upper classes but through various popular cultural forms from "Madonna's *Sex* book [1992] to K-mart *[sic]* Fetish perfume [1997]."[6] But the process began with Vivienne Westwood's groundbreaking " 'Sex,' a punk and fetish fashion boutique in London with Malcolm McLaren"[7] in the 1970s, accompanying the burst of antimodern, antitraditional fashion practice and antiestablishment political and social art forms that flourished in this time period. But Lehmann explains this phenomenon this way: "[F]ashion requires an element of alienation for its success. It has to appear not as something that develops organically but as an artificial creation. Its teleological origins always have to lie outside the culture, class, or social grouping that eventually adopts it."[8] That is to say, it is the exoticism of the stranger's work that provides the difference necessary for the concept of fashion, and more specifically, modern fashion, which requires the breath of the new to invigorate and "modernize" the object. Westwood, a rebel to the bone, found the S/M and DIY aspects of the British punk scene of the time compelling and sufficiently outrageous to adapt to her collection. Selling it in a boutique, also a new innovation of the time, placed her work at the vanguard of what was to become a major fashion tendency throughout the end of the twentieth century and would climax in the midpoint of the first decade of the twenty-first century.

As couture fashion entered the second decade of the twenty-first century, the weight of the pastiche of an ever-rotating array of historic fashions were brought to bear on postmodern fashion designers: Balenciaga, Herrera, McQueen, Wang, Galliano, Pugh, Gaultier, Valentino, LaCroix, and Westwood were but a few who quoted heavily from fetish as well as eighteenth- and nineteenth-century styles, particularly in their gowns, during this period. Also functioning as pastiches were the various decades of the twentieth century, particularly in the latter half. By around 2010, this obsession resulted in multiple details quoted from many decades collaged in a single work, creating a pastiche of class, cultures, and status. This mélange of styles is quoted so heavily and seemingly without any distinctions, yet it forms a sort of phantasmagoria, a term that Evans suggests has come to connote "some form of visual deception or display, in which shadowy and unreal figures appear only to disappear," but she also quotes Theodor Adorno as using the term "to designate the tricks, deceits and illusions of nineteenth century culture . . . whose near and far are deceptively merged"[9] in this fashion phenomenon. Questions arise from both critics and scholars as to the validity of a style seemingly based in pastiche, in the quotations of dead cultures, popular cultural icons, and the sexual apparatus of the fetish culture. Is Adorno correct? Is this a trick or deceit in which the past and the present *seem* to be merged but perhaps only as an illusion? Is this style simply a whirl of pastiche with an empty center? And if it is an illusion, why are we so tantalized by its spectacle?

A clue might be found in the discussion of the same phenomenon in pop music:

> Coined by the co-founders of cyberpunk fiction William Gibson and Bruce Sterling, "atemporality" is a term for the disconcerting absence of contemporaneity from so much current pop culture. This curious quality can be detected not just in pop music but in everything from fashion to graphic design to vintage chic.[10]

Sterling's sense of this "curious quality" comes from the onset of the digital culture, which has "dramatically increased the presence of the past in our lives . . . the sheer volume and range of back catalogue music, film, TV and so forth that is available for consumption is astounding."[11] These joint concepts of atemporality and phantasmagoria seem to describe the well-worn notion of the "network of signs," once the vanguard of the emerging postmodern technological culture, later accepted as the contemporary cultural form of communication in transnational cultures and economies. No longer the rational concept of the modernist "grid" in which objects sit in orderly relations, the postmodern formation is multilayered, dithering, unruly, and perverse. It is the past and present in a "deceptive merger" in which the modernist period, style, and fashion seem to have "jumped the shark"[12]—a television term to describe a moment when the narrative of a series that was once successful has reached a point where it must use extreme theatrical special effects, knuckle-headed slapstick, parody, sex, and spectacle in order to keep the interest of the audience. In a sense, postmodernity was/is modernity "jumping the shark": desperately at a loss for "the new," having spent all its assets in the twentieth century and finding no place in the technological and global maniacal explosion of Internet innovations of the twenty-first century to locate its narrative stalwarts of order or rationality, modernity relies only on a messy but massive network of DIY Internet expressions to pose as a form of "universality." Fashion has become the most prominent example of this structure, taking the spectacle to impossible heights as well as distancing itself all the more from the high modernist fashion standards of quality in cut and cloth.

Fetish in Fashion

> I was excited by this idea of taking culture to the streets and changing the whole way of life, using culture as a way of making trouble.
>
> Malcolm McLaren[13]

Corset

Valerie Steele attributes the first postmodern reappearance of the corset—as opposed to merry widows,[14] waist-cinchers, and other similar objects—to Vivienne Westwood in 1985; they were "inspired by eighteenth century stays, rather than the more familiar Victorian hourglass corset," and she states, "Fashion always requires something new yet draws from the past."[15] Robert Bell recalls,

> Westwood's subsequent collections, *Savage* (Spring/Summer 1982), *Buffalo* (Autumn/Winter 1982–83) and *Punkature* (Spring/Summer 1984), along with the opening of a second shop, *Nostalgia of Mud*, in 1982 explored the cultures of the Third World . . . and bizarre juxtapositions of under- and outerwear, corsets and brassieres . . . The corset emerged from this period as a key element in Westwood's language of forms, along with other historical body-shaping devices such as the crinoline, the bustle and the elevated shoe.[16]

This exploration of the body form, and the extent to which it can be altered for effect, became part of Westwood's feminist agenda. Freeing the female form from the boyish profile it had attained in the 1960s (Twiggy, for example), she mined the past for the ultrafeminine emphasis on the extreme curvaceous profile created by corsets, bustles, and petticoats of the eighteenth century. As Robert Bell notes, quoting Claire Wilcox:

> "In Westwood's clothes, sexuality is determined by sensation . . . her intention is arousal, both physical and mental, and to instill the wearer with the confidence that clothes bring not only to private and public pleasure but also an increased awareness through dressing up" . . . Westwood has continued to emphasize the idea of constriction as a way to define the body and its movement and to direct posture . . . she draws attention to the figure through exaggeration and distortion of the body shape.[17]

Westwood was a pioneer in the outing of both underwear and the effective aspect of fetish in fashion, beginning perhaps with her advice to young women to "Take your mother's old brassiere and wear it undisguised over your school jumper and have a muddy face!"[18] Although she used corsets primarily as a constrictive support in the early days, by the mid-1980s they were outside the gowns and sporting portraits—images from classical rococo paintings. In most of her evocations of the corset, she has alluded to the past in straightforward ways, although the context of the rest of the garment may diverge wildly from its founding quotation. In fact, most of her work is just such a mélange of quoted styles and fabrics pulled from different eras and disjointed uses as mentioned earlier. Yet the corset itself has been deconstructed: she tends to reveal and complicate the contradictions between its use as a tight-lacing machine and its visual allure through this functionless abbreviation of the actual object.

Fig. 5.1 One of Vivienne Westwood's many designs using corsets, at the Vivienne Westwood Ready to Wear Spring/Summer 2012 show during Paris Fashion Week at Grand Hotel Intercontinental on September 30, 2011. Photo by Antonio de Moraes Barros; courtesy of Filho/WireImage/Getty Images.

The corset has become in this work a mere sign of the corset, utterly non-functioning *except* as a sign—very much a device from the postmodern bag of tricks.

For Jean Paul Gaultier, the corset was only one aspect of fetish fashion that he has deployed as inspiration and intention in his work since 1985, when he introduced the cross-dressing "man-skirts" and henceforth produced "the label's gender-bending, deconstructed aesthetic, and risqué collaborations—like Madonna's infamous cone-shaped bra for the 1990 *Blonde Ambition* tour—[which] gave the designer his 'enfant terrible' reputation."[19] His designs show the corset not only in a somewhat traditional tight-lacing, eighteenth-century pastiche but also in an endless iteration of the garment in various reflections of popular cultural character forms, such as space aliens, pirates, and geisha. He also layers corsets in subtle soft leathers and synthetics as unique forms over coats, suits, dresses, and sportswear. The corset had by 2011 become de rigueur in his collections, and he cited the corset form in increasingly fantastic ways, playing with its implications of tight-lacing, fetish history and the feminine with his tongue firmly in his cheek.

Viktor & Rolf, during this same period, tended to use the corset in rather unremarkable, more traditional fashion. However, in 2007, they presented not a corset, but a constrictive mechanism that is reminiscent of the extreme forms of the fetish performance that extended from the corset-as-constriction S/M configurations (see Figure 4.3 in Chapter 4). A constrictive apparatus holding the model in place within a series of rather innocuous designs that tend to emulate the dresses of working women is seemingly extended from a collection of metal bars that infer a brace or even a surgically implanted position on/in the body of the model. The dresses are extended to the far edges of the apparatus, draped—rather than worn—over the model. Lights attached to the top of the apparatus are aimed at the model's face and glare down in a harsh spotlight. The metal rail upon which the stabilizing rails extend and the lights hang is connected—one must presume—to a track in the ceiling that allows the model attached to walk down the catwalk. No longer a "fashion" that one might purchase to wear, the design becomes art: a conceptual and highly political statement created as an imaginative work to articulate a critical judgment about the position of women in the workplace. The most salient aspect is the fetish implication of S/M, the tendency—in this case—toward a psychological condition for constriction, immobility, and domination, which women both desire and endure under the patriarchy. Viktor & Rolf wield their talents to propel their work beyond the design of mere fashion to the critique of societal norms. Blending the genres of critique and fashion is yet another symptom of the postmodern turn.

Dolce & Gabbana certainly seem to not only understand the attraction for constriction in fetish but also revel in a sometimes misogynous view of S/M. Apparent more from their infamous advertisements than from the actual designs, their acceptance of the mutable, erotic, and commodified nature of the female body emerges most succinctly in their corset designs. The most famous is the metal corset with *paniers*[20] of the 2006 collection. Designed to emulate the eighteenth-century undergarment, it was crafted of metal as a citation of the cyberpunk—a genre of science fiction in the late twentieth century set in a computer culture where humans emerged as "constructs" inside a computer landscape, forcing a cultural discussion of the "post-human," where the body was demoted to mere "meat." The S/M implications of the abjected human body became part of the postmodern discourse and had a tremendous effect on fashion in the first decade of the twenty-first century. It resulted in the adumbration of the "armored body" as a thematic force in the period fashions that was articulated in numerous fashions and narrative spectacles on the catwalk.

Fig. 5.2 Much like the hanging submissive of Jeroen van der Klis, this submissive is hanging from a light rail equipped with lights and cables during the Viktor & Rolf fashion show as part of Paris Fashion Week Autumn/Winter 2008 on February 26, 2007. Photo courtesy of Karl Prouse/Catwalking/Getty Images.

As Evans rightly observes,

For all its abject connotations, the fashion body could also survive pathology and abjection through the very process of reification, armouring itself through clothes, make-up and styling on the catwalk . . . armouring converts [the fashion body] into a fierce fetish, or charm: for if fetish is an object it is nevertheless a powerful one.[21]

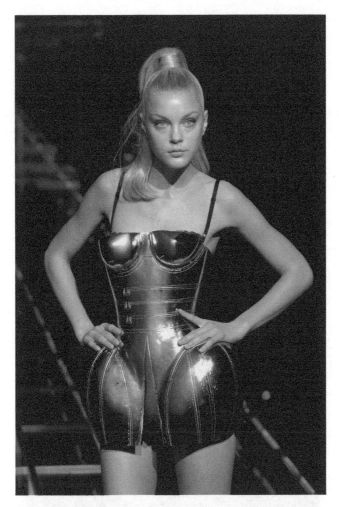

Fig. 5.3 Model Jessica Stam, wearing the corset made famous by Madonna, walks down the catwalk during the Dolce&Gabbana Fashion Show as part of Milan Fashion Week Spring/Summer 2007 on September 28, 2006. Photo courtesy of Chris Moore/Catwalking/Getty Images.

This notion of fashion as armor to protect the vulnerable "meat" body beneath—so feminized in modernity, so conspicuous as a commodity to manipulate, maneuver, and mutate to fit the market—became a place to critique these cultural hegemonies in this period's fashions. In their evocation of damaged and bleeding bodies and zombified expressions on the catwalk, a good number of designers adopted a disturbing tendency to mask the head in an array of forms to the obliteration of the model's face—the totem of humanity. This uncanny obsession is perhaps the most alarming, most transgressive citation of fetish practice—the abjection and negation of the animate individual human through masking.

Masks

The multitude of masks that proliferated in this particular moment—a moment seemingly obsessed with historic pastiche not only of form but of spectacle—are redolent

Fig. 5.4 A model walks down the catwalk wearing Gareth Pugh's square mask, utterly eliminating any human facial aspect, as part of London Fashion Week at the BFC Tent on September 16, 2007. Photo by Stuart Wilson; courtesy of Getty Images.

with a noir-esque preternatural sense of style. The masks are designed to represent the obfuscation of identity, but not just of individual identity; these masks are using overblown, amorphous, uncanny forms to obliterate human identity. Or perhaps, in the context of the post-human discourse, they are designed to enlarge the potential of human form: it is paradoxical, but not coincidental, that these two possibilities coexist. In fetish fashions, the mask also swivels in power, from the submissive to the dominant and back again: the master and the slave, the criminal and the superhero. It allows for the free play of character and identity and even species. In fashion, it theatricalizes and masks not only the model but the notion of the work as a part of the fashion design, and thus, a part of vocabulary of fashion forms. It proposes a character, with a dark history and dubious future. As the models walk down the catwalk, they are transposed from fashion models to characters in a drama.

The most compelling examples can be seen in the work of artists Gareth Pugh, Thierry Mugler, Junya Watanabe, and Jun Takahashi. Pugh, with his white plastic *commedia dell'arte* influences and abstract modernist sensibilities, creates masks that excuse the model from the human as they also set up an ironic turn through a sort of blank humor. His masks radically vary in form, from referencing a black plastic garbage bag that ties up at the top of the head, to a twinkling square or rhomboid, to a blown-up toy with minimal face that suggests Internet memes. Although each mask detracts from a human reference, each fashion below the mask still addresses the human form, but it is a costume: a garment designed for performance.

There seems to be a central clever joke to be gotten in Pugh's work, and it is found in his juxtapositions of contemporary culture and the value of the objects it produces. He masks his models in a foil to parry various cultural objects with the abstracted characters in the drama. In essence, he positions the objects as characters, paradoxically only masked as humans through the costumed human body. The commodities that crowd our existence have awoken with the eeriness of animate dolls. The layers of illusion unpack like this: the mask has an object identity juxtaposed with a human body that eternally pivots in a nanosecond's time—from object to human, from human to object—under which is a human who created the objects they enliven and who, as a subject of fashion and an identity as a fashion model, generates her condition as an object. That is, her humanity masks the conditions of the culture that also produce her as an object of fashion. Lehmann suggests a similarity to the goals of surrealism:

> The increased dominance of the object over the subject within the "tragedy of culture" . . . [imbues] humans with a mystery behind their outer appearance, [and] these artists had to find a way to make the mysterious become manifest. Unanimously, they chose clothes and accessories as symbolic of hidden fantasies and phantasmagories: close to the wearer's skin, yet nevertheless independent in its aesthetic and mythic expression.[22]

Although Lehmann was describing the surrealists in the early twentieth century, it certainly holds true for the surrealist designer-artists of contemporary postmodern

Fig. 5.5 A model walks the runway wearing a headdress that also masks the face created by Junya Watanabe, Fall/Winter 2008/2009 collection during Paris Fashion Week on February 26, 2008. Photo courtesy of Karl Prouse/Catwalking/Getty Images.

culture, who, just like the surrealists of the past, also sought to distort and morph the human form by masking it with the identity of objects.

Similar to surrealist works, Junya Watanabe's collection of 2008 presented a series of gowns in dark neutrals wrapped and overlapped to form an abstract sculptural swaddling effect that hugged the long, thin body of the model. Minimal yet expressive as it was abstract, the head was also swaddled in a black cloth that was carefully pulled, tucked, and stitched to reveal only the merest indication of a human face but pared down to the nose and vague suggestions of eyes along the brow. Attached to the head, seemingly growing out from the top like a massive industrial tumor, are vague but marvelous machine-like forms, like intellectual power tools extruding from the brain. The head of the model became a sculpture indicative of an obsolete industrial tool, though blackened with disuse over the passage of time, forgotten and dead. In fact, death is the character and identity of this mask; like a harbinger for our own time, it is an artifact that notes the passing of the post-hegemonic modern abstract industrial forms. The model beneath is a zombie, the walking dead, wrapped in a beautiful dark shroud, identity erased by death and—through the paradox of postmodern time—at once both ancient and contemporary.

The mask of Thierry Mugler appearing in his 2011 collection also signifies the death and life of the human. His mask relies on an evocative map of tattoos that reference the medical illustrations of the human head dissected and mapped with modernist "objectivity" in its fetishized lust for medical and scientific expertise. Yet beneath this medical determination of human construction is clearly the fully fleshed and somber face of the model. Animate, emotional, and alive, the face beneath bleeds through the death mask with a pathos of a subject who wears his own death's head as an emblem of the vulnerability of all things to change and transformation, as well as the folly and hubris of the modernist scientific fable of perfectibility. It fits into the domain of S/M through the fetish of science that has inscribed the evaluation of the human destiny onto the culture, making our dependence on science and medicine one of total submission to their agenda and manipulation. But it is also works in the reverse—just as in the fetish performance—in that the master becomes the slave; the face of the human under the domination of the mask enigmatically emerges to overwhelm the diagram with his unique and rebellious meanings, just as postmodern science realizes the importance of the context of human subjectivity, which also bleeds through the most "objective" scientist. Mugler, a genius in his haunting articulations of the postmodern, post-human condition and its contradictions and contrapuntal turns, seems to mirror Louis W. Marvick's insightful description of the French writer Fontenelle, also working in a similar time:

> By presenting the truth in the guise of a fable [he] excites the reader's mistrust; and that mistrust enforces the real lesson about the illusoriness, or at least, the incompleteness, of every truth we think we grasp . . . he excelled at working the surface, not as a means to an end in itself; or that he deliberately marred the *vraisemblance* [the probability or plausibility] at the very moment when, by art that hides itself, he might have induced the reader to believe that he had found the truth.[23]

That is to say, Mugler and the other fashion mask-makers, rather than performing mere acts of fashion, are actually using fashion as commentary and using the illusionary and provocative device of the mask to critique the cultural issues that confront the possibility of the truth of the "master narratives" of modernist culture. Further, by using fashion itself (considered a practice concerned simply with "surface" issues

Fig. 5.6 A model presents a floral profusion as mask created by Japanese designer Jun Takahashi for Undercover during the Spring–Summer 2005 Ready to Wear collections presentations in Paris on October 4, 2004. Photo courtesy of Pierre Verdy AFP/Getty Images.

and commodity goals) and by using this sort of work—fashion—as an "art that hides itself" under its blatant commodious ontological signification, these designers put these things together to make it a contradictory and unexpected event and actually get the message to the observer with more significance and belief in its "truth." Fashion is using the illusion, surface, fatuity, and its nature as a product in the market to attempt to do the same thing that art is supposedly doing: critiquing the culture through a symbolic and sensual means.

Finally, in one of the most reproduced images of postmodern fashion's obsession with masking, Jun Takahashi's 2006 Fall/Winter Undercover Show "is widely regarded as Takahashi's breakout collection: the model's bodies and faces were completely covered; jackets were wrapped and bandaged together, while faces were completely shrouded in mummified masking." Takahashi explained, "Why did I cover everything up? There was no reason, except to efface all feeling, like a destroyed doll."[24] Of course, to "efface all feeling" is a loaded goal, one that landed like an explosion on the scene in 2006. But he also told Suzy Menkes, " 'There is no reason to think about it—it comes naturally' . . . 'It is not a question of appearances—it is more about a feeling,' he explains."[25] What may seem to be a contradictory statement actually speaks, once again, to the postmodern concern with pastiche and the post-human. Takahashi's mask is a pastiche of a burka, a "type of veil and body covering [that] conceals all of a woman's body including the eyes, which are covered with a mesh screen. Common in Afghanistan; sometimes refers to the 'niqab' face veil."[26]

Itself misunderstood though extensively written about, the veil that Islamic women wear is in devotion to Islamic law, but it was also discussed as a fetishized (by the French military) "revolutionary covering" during the Algerian War.[27] Takahashi's work is an aesthetic choice based in "feeling." His veil/mask takes on the appearance of the burka but with the punk embellishments of many randomly placed clumps of safety pins, hooked together in tandem and pinned to piles of fabric wrapped around the tripartite hood and mask forming a high headpiece suggestive of African women's headpieces. Intricate silver necklaces extend from the hooded mask in long strands that seem to be wrapped around the model's shoulders. The middle part of the tripartite mask bears the perforated screen that is reminiscent of the eye screen on the burka. Takahashi seems to be bringing the heavily disputed issues of immigration, difference, and human rights of the West—particularly French issues with Islamic student veiling in France—into discursive play within the very territory of French hegemony: fashion. Interestingly, as he told *Vogue* about this "Beautiful V" collection: "There are two ways of eroticism: to cover up or to show. Undercover [Takahashi's design firm] is anti-showing off . . . I like to break the rules," he said. "I get my ideas from life's mysterious dark side. That has been the basis for Undercover and the meaning behind the name since the very beginning."[28] He recognizes and subversively propels forward the missing, unmentioned issue that lurks behind the colonial discourse around the veiling issue: the eroticism of the veil—or mask. Once again, we are brought back into the realm of S/M and the power valence of master/slave, perhaps the reason the French military feared the veils of the Algerian women.

Takahashi uses the atemporality and the spectacle of phantasmagoria in the presentation of his work: he counters his own feelings with a goal of a lack of feeling, the past with the present, the West with the East, and the power valence that has developed in these postmodern collisions with the force of the explosive spectacle of phantasmagoria in fashion—safer than military collisions, and stronger. This particular image of his mask became "viral" on the Internet precisely because of its stunningly dark, unnerving power to bring to bear the myriad discursive strands of discourse in the areas that we are afraid to see. The veil translates culturally in different ways in East and West, but it pivots around the disputed rights and erotic powers of women using the ubiquitous yet dominant leverage of fashion. The perversity of the image is secured through a bewitching nimbus of eroticism and the paradoxical play between master and slave of S/M.

Bondage

The bondage of S/M and the pleasure and pain of constriction are evidenced in the predilection for various strappings and bindings that appear in fashion during the first

Fig. 5.7 Trussed up in the bondage-strapped corset of Alexander McQueen, a model walks the runway at the Alexander McQueen fashion show during Paris Fashion Week on March 8, 2011. Photo courtesy of Karl Prouse/ Catwalking/Getty Images.

decade of the twenty-first century. It appears in mild implications of shoe straps, strapped leggings, and corset straps and as detail on outerwear. But perhaps the most virulent and sustained use of explicit fetishistic bondage appears in Alexander McQueen's 2011 collection, which was clearly influenced by the fetish wear of the dominatrix. Most evocations of his bondage designs appear on what might be described as "harnesses." These harnesses enclose the body from the waist and appear to be of a singular design. Made from stiff black leather, they are sometimes ornamented with various sorts of studs, buckles, and metal strips. Some harnesses also extend around the shoulder, creating a further vision of constriction. Others have "breast plates" of leather that are attached to straps extending from the choker neck strap and running down the center of the chest, and they are also attached to side straps extending up from the front waist, which wrap up and over the shoulders to the waist in back. This harness is somewhat similar for all the works in this collection, but the garment under the straps differs, from a white evening dress, to a black leather dominatrix/business suit, to a corset and skirt. Other designs include bondage straps on an ornate rococo black leather leaf-textured gown, implied straps on jackets and dresses using black fabric and zippers, and straps encircling thigh-high boots that lace from the toes to the thighs. McQueen is clearly citing the fetish costumes of the dominatrix, in a fashion that rivals only Thierry Mugler and Dolce&Gabbana for its authenticity to fetish costume and explicit S/M meanings. But virtually every designer in the early twenty-first century has straps that bind somewhere in some way and signify bondage in their collections.

Skinsuits

Skinsuits, also in the constriction category, appeared in many collections in the postmodern period, in various manifestations: some designers reflect only the innovations made in synthetic production, but others have responded with overt citation of fetish use in constriction and character play. Gareth Pugh seems to be more involved with the manifestation of character in his skinsuits, and indeed, in most of his work. Most directly evocative of the fetish skinsuit is a red maillot that leaves the legs and one arm bare and is hooded or masked with what is explicitly a fetish hood. The hood sports only one eye and has the signature round, open mouth, usually for effectuation in sexual fetish play. However, his addition of plastic balls of varying sizes, which appear on the side of the head, right below the left breast, and on the sleeved right arm, reflects his sense of humor. The skinsuit is entirely covered in round plastic disks that emulate goose bumps. It seems Pugh is having a bit of fun with the fetishists, creating a fetish of "balls" at peculiar locations, complete with mock evidence of excitation. The plain, short black boots also frame this design as a parody, rather than the thigh-high laced black leather boots that are indicative of the serious business of the dominatrix—we become the submissive in being the subject of the joke. Pugh is clearly cognizant of the predilection for the couture and the emerging independent designers' use of fetish pastiche in the work of this period. And he cannot seem to help himself from having a satiric "go" at them.

In another work, however, he uses the skinsuit as a structural foil in the *commedia dell'arte*–influenced collection of 2008, in which he quotes details from the styles of the seventeenth-century costumes of "Pierrot and Pierrette," but abstracted and simplified down to a construction of many white strips on a black background; these are placed in a grid fashion and, in so doing, flatten the costume and force a connection to a sort of "space suit" version reminiscent of the minimalist works of the late twentieth century. It is a prime example of the "piling up of pastiche" to effect an appearance that oscillates from century to century, and from character to character, creating a hybrid that twinkles in its presentation with the various facets of its origins and effects. Each design in this collection seems to carry some, but not all, of the devices of this symptom of postmodernity. It is the character of Pierrot and Pierrette but only for an instant before it signifies another character or time, creating the sort of atemporality that is engendered from a constellation of fashion quotations ever-swiveling in signification and a phantasmagoria of multiple signs.

Jean Paul Gaultier, also enjoying the open season on parody and phantasmagoria and long known for his frequently humorous theatrical displays of past centuries and sexual innuendos, uses all the tricks in the book when designing. The skinsuit is no exception. His elaboration of the skinsuit stretches across many centuries and multitudes of characters, all done with panache and humor mixed into a single collection, yet it signals the cultural commentary on fashion and fetish with direct confrontations of stereotypes and erotic desire. In one instance, he comments on the "Audrey Hepburn-type" in her *Breakfast at Tiffany's* manifestation. He totally encloses the figure down to her fingertips in a skinsuit of hound's-tooth check, superbly tailored and complete with the signifying "props" of the cigarette holder, the sunglasses, the purse, and the umbrella—all entirely upholstered in the hound's-tooth check. The clearly fetishistic facial delineation of the mask—with which we are now familiar—is complete with eyeholes and the open mouth, signifying the penetrable subject. He stretches the notion of the skinsuit to include the fashion props that become part of her skin in the evocation of this character, and therein lies the "punctum" of this design.

This reference to "type" works as a character fetish: in the fetishizing of a narrative, the dreaming subject fetishizes the costume and performance of this character-within-a-scene as it supplies *jouissance*. In so doing, the fetishizing allows the scene to become salient in terms of the subject's desire and to literally stand in for the fulfillment either of a sexual act or of power and/or identity. Gaultier completely understands the desire of the fashionista, who longs for the sophistication, money, and power to be an Audrey Hepburn—to have the perfect pert little body and face, to be beloved of fashion designers and the public, to be sophisticated and wealthy, to not only be able to own and wear couture fashion but be the "darling" of her favorite designer, and to live the life of the true fashionista. The profundity of the level of desire

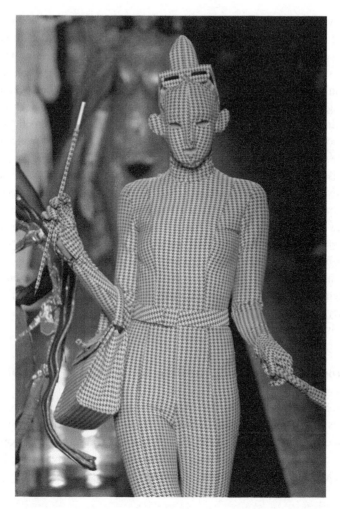

Fig. 5.8 Channeling Audrey Hepburn in *Breakfast at Tiffany's*, a model walks down the catwalk in a catsuit during the Jean Paul Gaultier Retro Fashion Show as part of Paris Fashion Week Spring/Summer 2007 on October 3, 2006. Photo courtesy of Karl Prouse/Catwalking/Getty Images.

for this sort of fetish cannot be overestimated: many, many women participate the world over in this sort of dream and create elaborate behaviors and make purchases in an attempt to actuate—just as do the sexual fetishists—their dream of fulfillment, to the delight and profit of capitalistic corporations.

In another case, Gaultier also "plays" on the unspoken, subtextual mechanisms implicit in the design of couture designs, and gowns in particular, of profoundly erotic sexuality and the appearance of wealth and luxury as indications of power and class. In particular, this skinsuit is designed to exemplify the body of an actual nude woman—the

breasts, navel, and pubic area of which are articulated in a somewhat realistic fashion—while the skin is of a shimmering golden transparent fabric dotted with small
round dots of gold, and the costume is topped with long opera gloves of bright gold.
The nipples are cast in a darkened gold while at the groin, a hilarious overgrown dark-
black "bush" of curly pubic hair sprouts enthusiastically. Underneath the pubic area, a
white triangle of underwear can just be seen to hide the model's own hair, suggesting
more succinctly the performative "costume" aspect rather than a mimetic attempt at
a human skin. Over her shoulders hangs a satiny golden trench coat, which seals the
clever joke Gaultier has wickedly implanted in this design.

And this joke works on several levels: primarily, it is an ironic play on the idea of
the male exhibitionist, a type of fetishist who typically hides his naked body under
a trench coat with clip-on trouser legs in order to reveal himself unexpectedly in a
public area to women and girls and thus achieve orgasm.[29] But on a secondary level,
it also refers to the exhibitionist as the sophisticated woman of fashion "dressed to
kill" who parades her fashion-forward self in public areas, becoming—or so the
fetishistic narration goes—the object of desire for all who see her (and thus perhaps
she also achieves orgasm). Gaultier's knowledge of human eroticism in all its humor,
eccentricity, absurdity, and beauty are the tools in his design kit, and in this particular
venue, he is the master.

The "Fancy Movement" and the Designer of Popular Cultural Fetish

So far, we have been discussing the couture designers and their relationships with,
perceptions of, and interpretations of fetish in their work. But there are an increasing
number of emerging designers and styles from the vast realms of global popular cultures, now connected intimately through the Internet, that are establishing fetishistic
styles that also influence the fashions of couture. It begins in "cosplay":

> Purportedly originating in Japan in 1978 with a performance by Mari Kotani parodying
> either a manga or anime character, fan performances of popular cultural narratives seem to
> have welled up in various parts of the world around that time. At 1960s sci-fi conventions,
> Star Trek fans had begun to dress as their beloved characters and . . . continue to do so
> even now . . . Online legend has it that Nov Takahashi saw Star Trek costumes worn at the
> 1984 Los Angeles Science Fiction Worldcon and coined the term *kosu-pure* (コスプレ).[30]

Cosplay, or "costume-play," began as a much-maligned and ignominious practice
among the fans of certain television series, beginning with Star Trek. However, once
anime first began to appear in the United States in the late 1980s, fans there began to
arrive at Star Trek conventions in anime costumes, appearing first at the San Diego
Comic-Con Convention in 1979.[31] The Japanese have used the originally denigrating
term *otaku* to designate these fan populations of anime, manga,[32] and gaming that

have adopted a regime of obsessive fetishistic and ritual behavior by celebrating these narratives with specific fan behaviors, most notably cosplay. Consequently, a community has developed around the desire and yearning "of" and "for" the popular cultural characters of these narratives.[33] Yet *otaku*, and especially the *shôjo*—the extremely popular young girl of manga and anime with her infamous reputation for "pornographic" works that deal especially in *Yaoi*, or "Boy Love," stories of male homosexual love and sex in particular—are in fact an abjected population, not only representing Kristevian abjection but in the very everyday and poignant sense of the word. Within their abject profile and community, these subjects have accumulated a cornucopia of identities that have been imaginatively suggested by anime and manga and mirror the lack of fixed identities, gender roles, and sexualities through costuming.

However, cosplay was not initially design: it was the mimetic adoption of existing designs found in manga and anime. Steele notes that "Japanese Vogue has also explored the relationship between fashion and manga, . . . [and] juxtaposed runway photographs of European fashions with manga images."[34] But there emerged other related costume design movements brought on by cosplay. Most notable was the Lolita movement, which grew from the *zoku*, or tribes, of costumed character players who began to appear in Tokyo's Harajuku neighborhood in the 1990s. They have evolved globally into a wide variety of genres—Classic Lolita, Sweet Lolita, Gothic Lolita, Aristocratic Lolita, and more—as they developed their global membership. As they progressed, designers appeared, beginning with their most famous store, Baby, The Stars Shine Bright, founded in 1988 by Akinori Isobe. The movement quickly expanded into other brands: Angelic Pretty, Alice and the Pirates, Juliette and Justine, and Victorian Maiden.[35]

The Lolita extends from *shôjo* culture but centers specifically on one of the last bastions of mythic femininities of the patriarchic culture. Performed initially almost entirely by women, but increasingly also by men, the Lolita is a costumed performance of various fetishized character types based on the appearance of the somewhat fictionalized Victorian notion of the "little girl." The Lolita, as a female playing a female, sets up a condition where an absence, gap, or denial of a core femininity is implied:

> We can read the paradox of the shōjo in the various permutations of Lolita ("Loli") cosplay . . . The process of "dressing-up" is a variation on the popular pastime of little girls and explains something of the allure of the shôjo culture . . . Adopting the morphology of the abject state through Loli cosplay, the body is supplanted by an imaginary identity and body form through the application of a costume and character from one of the Loli genres, a process which also serves to elide the founding condition of the abject body. In Loli cosplay, these obsessions also proliferate around the form and fabric details of Victorian fashions and subject positions, which in contemporary culture are understood as decidedly fetishistic.[36]

This fetish style has been catapulted to a global scope, and members of the Lolita community can be found in virtually every country with an Internet connection.

Fig. 5.9 Three key designers and remarkable women of the Lolita style are, from left to right, Samantha Rei of Blasphemina's Closet, Megan Bishop of Apatico, and Heather Luca of Scoundrelle's Keep. Photo courtesy of Drayke Larson of Photosynthetique.

In its constant evolution, the "lifestyle Lolita" has appeared as a particularly compelling group, organized and proliferated through Facebook and other online alliances; these women—many beyond their twenties—have begun to wear modified Lolita fashions in their everyday life. Consequently, lifestyle Lolita designers have appeared who design not just for costume play of imagined identity but for women in their daily lives. Samantha Rei, of Blasphemina's Closet, is just such a designer. She has been designing, showing, and selling Lolita designs since 2000:

> Pulling inspiration stemming from historical fashion, fairytales and Japanese youth fashion . . . make[ing] one-of-a-kind pieces, custom projects, wedding gowns and high-end items. Samantha draws her inspiration from such illustrators and *[sic]* Chris Riddell, Brom, Tony DiTerlizzi, Brett Helquist and Mihara Mitsukazu as well as stories like *Alice in Wonderland* and *Snow White*. Her hero Alexander McQueen as well as designers Vivienne Westwood, H. Naoto, John Galliano, Colleen Atwood, and Victorian Maiden have [also] influenced her style.[37]

Rei has become a leader in this phenomenon, with followers from all over the world, and has initiated its title as the "Fancy Movement." Steampunk and other Victorian costume movements are quickly growing as the Fancy Movement proliferates. Other designers such as Heather Luca, corset designer of Scoundrelle's Keep, and Megan

Bishop, hatmaker of Apatico,[38] who are associates of Rei, have formed the leading wave of the movement in the United States. Rei, now in association with another leading Lolita designer, Megan Maude, has created a new line:

> Luxette (a portmanteau of the words "luxury" and "coquette"; not to be confused with "luxe grunge") is a modern subculture fashion . . . as a way to protest the mass-market clothing worn by youth in the early 2000s and a way to bring back "classic beauty" . . . its aesthetic [is] deeply rooted in 18th and 19th century clothing as well as fashions from the 1920s–1960s. Megan and Samantha viewed the current trends in fashion as "lazy due to the need for inexpensive instant gratification . . . Luxettes (and their male counterparts Luxeurs), care deeply about beauty, modesty, class, libertinism, art and indulgence."[39]

Rei and her associates have also staged costume-themed parties under the umbrella group called "Libertine Asylum." She was influenced in this event by the remarkable costume-themed events to be found in New York City several times a month called "Dances of Vice":

> The creation of Shien Lee, "Dances of Vice" is a New York nightlife sensation which attracts a decadent menagerie of dandies, aesthetes, and dreamers who gather in shared enthusiasm for the music, fashion, culture, and beauty of times forgotten. "Dances of Vice" incorporates a myriad of anachronistic and New Romantic influences in Dadaistic celebration of the liberating effects of beauty, fantasy and surrealism.[40]

Each event is concocted by the amazing Shien Lee, the mysterious and beautiful young Taiwanese entrepreneur who produces and emcees the events, and whose enigmatic allure and seemingly exhaustive closet of costumes colors each theme: "Alice in Wonderland," "Harlem Renaissance," "Shangai *[sic]* Foxtrot," "Dot, Dot, Dot," "Viper's Dream," "Disco Nouveaux," and "Le Poisson Rouge." Everyone dresses in an array of outstanding costumes, most homemade but some purchased at high prices, that more or less follow the theme of the event. The live music, dancers, burlesque performances, and dealers all are evocative of the theme. Many people attend these lush events, all in costume, all masked, all celebrating not just the fetish thrill of crossing gender, but also the *jouissance* of becoming an Other. This allows the performance of an imagined luxury and refinement, of stories of the demimonde, of romantic nights in silks and satins, dancing and drinking in an altered world, in an atemporal moment, embedded deep, deep into the phantasmagoric experience. It is the apex of the Fancy Movement: a defiant act against the American fetish for a prolonged adolescence, evidenced in grown men, and some women, whose uniform is a horror of grubby cargo shorts or ratty jeans, oversized faded T-shirts and the dirty trainers or flip-flops seen on any weekend on the bulk of the American middle class, who refuse to change from this costume for theater, church, or any public event. The Fancy Movement is a call for fashion, in its expanded global and popular forms, to radically alter the world.

Fig. 5.10 Impresario Shein Lee poses in eighteenth-century costume at one of the famous and very hip "Dances of Vice" events in New York City. Photo courtesy of Pierre Leszczcyk of EmpireArt.

Yet another source of fetish fashion can be found in the illustrators of fetish, those who are able not just to create images of existing fetish fashions but also to comprehend the sensual and sexual aspects of fetish so well that they can amplify the intensity of the fetish expression through the imaginative, impossible projection of fantasy costumes. Hajime Sorayama of Japan, arguably the foremost illustrator of fetish, creates pinup girls, in the manner of Vargus; but instead of his warm, pink healthy-looking young girls, Sorayama's are strong, disdainful, and, many times, cybernetic dominatrices. These are fashions only for the mind to wear, propelling, augmenting, and intensifying the potential of a costume to sport accoutrement perhaps not possible and certainly difficult to wear. Sorayama's skinsuit in Figure 5.11 is redolent with the influence of cyberpunk and flourishes an array of sexual implements. Sorayama explains that he "produces what is impossible"; since his "art is does not assume real use, he can do what he wants, and his impossible imagination is what attracted fetishists in Europe."[41] He explains that because of the current Gothic Lolita phenomenon, there is a lack of a more traditional fetish culture in Japan. Further, because the *otaku* culture fetishizes and collects actual things, the fetishist must collect things that do not exist. Sorayama enjoys the juxtaposition and irony of conjoining the possible with the impossible in his designs. He uses light, transparency, and reflection as his aesthetic,

Fig. 5.11 An imaginative painting (c. 1990) by the remarkable artist and illustrator Hajime Sorayama, who designs for dreams and desires not attainable on earth. Courtesy of Sorayama/Uptight Co., Ltd. 2012, www.sorayama.com.

producing skinsuits that gleam with a metallic sheen, which greatly enhances the forms and shapes of fetish desire. He knows that women are attracted to fabric that is soft like a baby's skin, so he uses this light-infused metallic illusion to effect a sensual, sexual response. He believes that "the aim of art is to amaze people, to lead them to places they have not been. To astonish people as a form of communication through the shock of the sensual recognition."[42]

Other illustrators who create the fantasy forms that can be considered fetish fashions are Brom, Michael Manning, and Sardax. But most illustrators of fetish are much more about the nude body in bondage or in another act of fetish fulfillment.

Even those illustrators listed here who do some design of garments do not do what Sorayama does: they do not compete with fashion designers. Sorayama's stated goal is to surpass the fashion designers he admires and is inspired by. His links to the fashion world are strong, and his work reveals the marvelous and impossible beauty that fetish can inspire.

–6–

The Future of Fetish Style:
"The Play's the Thing"

In addition to a great amount of self-conscious artifice, the aesthetic figurae of the baroque manner include many scopic/observational devices such as the conceit, repetition, parody, the Menippean satire, carnivalization, metamorphoses, metalepses, intertextuality, the encyclopedia, cataloging, mirroring, trompe l'oeil, the labyrinth, staging, distortion, contradiction, instability, disorder, chaos, detail, and fragment.

Cristina Degli-Esposti, "Sally Potter's *Orlando* and the Neo-Baroque Scopic Regime"[1]

The demand to posit a "future" for any human endeavor—but particularly for humans involved in attempting to stage and consequently fulfill human desire—is daunting; and although in some ways the future is predictable, using that "predictability" can also prove the folly of hubris. However, there are one or two things that will be true in the future: first, human beings exist in a narrative form of consciousness: in language, in dreams, in memory, and particularly in desire. We will always need to consider and articulate our desires through a narrative. The characters and style of the mise-en-scène of these dramas will be based on human experiences of the past—whether of one's own past or the historical cultural past. We can also say that the fetish narratives developed in modernity have lasted to the present, with changes occurring only through the bounties gained in technologies and innovations during the modern period. The formulaic narratives of fetish desire seem to sustain a certain stability through time, as do their fashions that were developed to intensify desire. In fact, one of the primary curiosities in this work was the rigorous durability of the dominatrix costume and its Victorian codes for over a century. Fashion can also be depended upon to reflect the cultural discourses in which it emerges, now and, one can only presume, in the future.

Yet there are other, more worldly things about this complex of signs and functions appearing under the term *fetish* that one could also predict for the future:

The tendency to "re-present," as Gilles Deleuze would have it, the forms of the past appears more strongly when disorder and decline force a confused, contradictory state of mind, when the only certainty is that everything is uncertain, when the desire to impress and shock through massiveness and grandeur appears to be a way out. This has occurred at many other times in history, and we see it happening today in many postmodern artistic expressions.[2]

Deleuze recognized the tendency of history to rely on the "grandeur" of past periods, when in the decline of its civilization, a culture "jumps the shark" in seeking a style to keep itself together, to muster a sense of fashion that can masquerade the tottering culture as opulent and stable. Mannerism is that eccentric and much maligned style first identified in the painters of the late Renaissance—who took to painting " 'alla maniera di,' that is, 'in the manner of' the great artists of the Renaissance"³—which was replaced and disregarded by the baroque as it sashayed into the culture following the mannerist moment. Mannerism becomes a bridge over two epistemes, to use a Foucaultian term. It is a masquerade that borrows from the past—the fashions of success, wealth, and stability—and masks both the decay of the previous episteme and the onset of the new forms, practices, and philosophies. It works literally as a bridge: a passage on which the societies under reconstruction are allowed to make their messy transitions, their transformations and changes along with the accompanying emotional outbursts of fear and trepidation, in a space wherein the comforting recognition of past forms eases an acceptance of the new regimes. Ihab Hassan has also recognized the tendency to observe this mannerist implication in the postmodern culture:

> Analysis of a historical situation or cultural style does not imply a "definition" of either; at best, we reach some working consensus about terms like "modernism," a consensus continually subject to critical revisions . . . Nor will postmodernism be defined except as a shifting matrix of ideas, a moot consensus, which may or may not harden some day into a term like "baroque" or "mannerism." But the "softness" of postmodernism as concept does not indicate its nugacity. Quite the opposite is the case: soft concepts generate interesting, heuristic, and productive debates.⁴

Hassan also recognizes the beneficial aspects of the "interesting, heuristic, and productive debates" in the continuing discussions of the postmodern turn as it glides from the manic late twentieth-century representations to its maturing forms found in the early twenty-first century. The lack of solid ground generates a plethora of compelling practices, which in this period come together in the increasing incidents of theatrical events.

The appearance of fetish performances in mainstream culture came through the fashions of those performances. This is documented earlier, in the work of Vivienne Westwood and Malcolm McLaren in the early 1970s creating fetish punk; Leigh Bowery's unique designs of non-gendered, body-morphing, carnivalesque self-representation in the mid-1980s; and also Jean Paul Gaultier's and John Galliano's bricolage of historic forms and the club culture in London that revolutionized fashion for decades to come. It was in the fashion shows of those designers and others that the performance of *fashion-as-fetish* came "out of the closet" and into mainstream culture. Jameson's fearful enlightenment-based admonitions—like those of many other critics of that time—can be read in his commentary on these events. In 1984,

Fig. 6.1 A performance as fashion show—a fashion show as performance. Alexander McQueen's last collection was shown during the 2010 CFDA Fashion Awards at Alice Tully Hall at Lincoln Center on June 7, 2010, in New York City. He was a genius who brought a little more glamour to the world and will be sorely missed. Photo courtesy of Andrew H. Walker/Getty Images.

he wailed that "history was being plundered in contemporary visual culture to make a post-modern carnival, and that the incessant return to the past was itself a kind of deathly recycling of history which emptied it of meaning, rendering it bankrupt, good only for costume drama and fantasy"[5]—"like it was a bad thing," as we say in the United States. For the modern men of that time, it signaled a "deathliness" (of the modern period's patriarchy), a "recycling of history" (as if it had never been done before, yet somehow we survived), which, they felt, "emptied it of its meanings" (that is, its *modernist* meanings) and "rendered it bankrupt" (of their masculinist modernist chilly goals of universality, purity attained through mathematics and science, formality through abstraction and simplification, and the hegemonies of the West, the white, the heterosexual, and the "new"). While men in the early modern world represented the "new" modern individual, women remained as representations of the past. Consequently, this postmodern return to past styles has meant a threatening loss of a masculine predominance and a dangerous insinuation of the feminine for the modern man.

For the young and the other marginalized people of that time, it was liberation. From the rigidity of the modernist regime came a riot of celebratory fashions and fashion shows. Fetish fashions released both men and women from the confines of the modern, but they also released the Others: the homosexuals, the transsexuals, the cross-dressers, and all those that defy categorization from their third-class closets. Although fetish fashion was considered transgressive, intimidating, and "good only for costume drama and fantasy," costume drama and fantasy were precisely what occurred. The new clarion of the Internet blew out these new fashion celebrations and styles around the world, and the world responded with its own versions. Thus the world changed, and we entered the mannerist passage toward a future that looms ahead.

What does the "future"—currently backlit as a reflection and criticism of the present—reveal to us? I believe it includes a transformation in the notion of identity. We tend to speak of our identity as a singular, unified, and unchanging entity. But the rage for costume play and celebration seems to suggest that something is happening to that notion. The notion of a singular identity arrived just as psychology and psychiatry were formed in the late nineteenth century, part of the modernist formation, wherein gender prescribed both roles and identities for subjects. This proliferation of gendered categories, replete with the strict definitions, rules, and regulations guarding the boundaries of social performance, makes costume play indicative of the profound changes emerging in popular culture around the presentation, performance, and citation of subjects and their genders.[6]

Through the specific aspects of the costume, the performer creates an occasion for the citation of hypostatized identity and genders gleaned in postmodernity from popular cultural narratives. The costumed identity becomes a series of "snapshots" of shifting identity illusions made possible by the release of the founding identity under the mask: it is a flickering series of momentarily stabilized characters that are fundamentally unstable. The actual mechanism by which the subject performs her or his disappearing act in the calling forth of multiple and oppositional roles[7] is lived and performed in a netherworld of multiple, fantastical, and potential identities. This is the place where it all happens as desire blossoms into the negotiation. Irony and paradox erupt in the moment of simultaneous play between the normative and the subversive, the self and the character, the normative gender roles with the renegade, and the multiple subjectivities and desires; this spawns not a singular performed identity or role but a shimmering multitude of desires and identities that I am identifying—after Félix Guattari—as the *transversal* moment. Bryan Reynolds, who has created an acting technique based on this concept, defines it this way:

> Transversal theory maintains that people occupy subjective territories, their own as well as through various kinds of sharing and overlappings. Subject territories are multidimensional, combined conceptual, emotional, and physical ranges of experience . . . its boundaries continue to be permeable and fluid insofar as imagination is capable of exceeding social, biological, and physical constraint and mutability is possible for all things.[8]

I began to receive this insight while watching cosplayers at anime conventions, not only as they performed in the regulated events but also as they wandered around in the hallways, conglomerating together, posing, voguing, and inter*acting* with the other cosplayers and convention attendees. It became clear that they no longer—if they ever did—were acting "in character": instead, they were slipping and sliding into all manner of identities that have no name but are identifiable through their rapid-fire snippets of gestures, manic vocal peculiarities, and poses, to become popular cultural iconic characterizations and quotations of exotic, erotic, and gendered types. This display of multiple identity eruptions begins precisely as the costume is put on and the subject encounters other cosplayers. At once the subject expands to the transversal position: "Transitional phenomena occur in an 'intermediate area of experience' and a 'potential space' . . . Transversality holds open this 'potential space' of creativity and collectivity."[9]

The notion of collectivity is key to understanding the potential space held within the transversal state: the fetish of cosplay is about the performer *and* the audience simultaneously. Cosplay is almost always a group activity at conventions. Even if the cosplayer arrives alone, he or she is immediately brought into the community of cosplayers and begins to act as performer *and* audience. Cosplaying starts with the desire to find community for the abject individual. This netherworld—this non-local local space of possibilities and multiplicities of potential that exists as the transversal— is created by the intensely felt bonds of the community, which not only allows for these performances but seeks them out simultaneously to perform and to watch almost constantly throughout the convention period.[10] The exact same conditions hold true for both the fetish performance and the attendee of the fashion show.

Costume play of the postmodern period—whether cosplay, fashion, or fetish performance, but perhaps less so in the fashion show—is created by an abject community and plays a vital role in the life of such groups as the missing *jouissance*. It not only informs their fantasy life but it also re-creates and extends it through the performances of these "potential new subjectivities" that are translated through the texts of popular culture. Characters as constructs created in costume play, but acting as aspects of the subject, are indeed what is *real* for the subject. They perform because new subjectivities provide the pleasures and acceptance lacking in the mainstream culture. It is therapeutic: "[I]t is, rather, a space in which becomings are truly creative—radically open and simply not what is now actual."[11]

As a culture, we tend to think and speak of the identity of ourselves and of others in the singular number: each person as a singular and unique *identity*. But it is becoming evident that what we conceive of as a distinct and particular singularity is in fact a multitude of identity affects and desires that swirl in constellations within each individual psyche, which the ego then creates situationally into identity formations. These formations construct aspects, desires, and affects for each social and nonsocial event—and through time and situation condense these aspects, desires, and affects into sets of successful traits that we then read as a singular whole identity or "self." These psychic landscapes form what we then perceive to be ourselves and others. But this has been because identity could *only* be read as the modernist binaried individual singular: we currently have had no model of a subject that could accommodate a subjectivity with the potential multiplicity of identifying traits as still fluid, still potential, and contingent—and still be considered sane.[12] It is the key reason that fetishists *must* conceive of themselves as a character in a drama, rather than the integrated aspect of their desire, and consequently must perform their desire in a theatrical paraspace, in costume as someone else—a character, not the self—being played by the subject.

According to Michel Foucault's construct, modernist institutions and prohibitions had provided a particular set of rules that closed down what could be thought or said, privileging the singular masculine subject. Fetish performance was outed by Vivienne Westwood and Malcolm McLaren in the late 1970s as the postmodern discourse entered its most productive stage. This is coincident with the beginning phase of the globalization of fashion culture through the development of fan groups and various exchange systems on the Internet, making fashion and, indeed, fetish accessible to mainstream global communities. The postmodern paradigm shifted constructs of subjectivity to consider potential pluralities of class, genders, and sexualities. Additionally, with the shifting focus toward the marginal, the culture began to realign what was seeable and sayable—if only for the emergent youth affiliations of the time. Foucault defined this process as the "technologies of the self," describing it as follows:[13]

> The way in which the subject constitutes himself in an active fashion, by the practices of the self, these practices are nevertheless not something that the individual invents by himself. They are patterns that he finds in his culture and which are proposed, suggested, and imposed on him by his culture, his society and his social group.[14]

It seems as if what the future may hold for the relationship between fetish and fashion is to be one of integration on several different levels. First, for the subjects involved with fetish, is perhaps an integration of their desire with themselves—not as characters in a drama but as aspects of their own desire. Also, the secret "night world" of their desires—still understood by most people as subversive and perverse—might at one point in the future be better understood, and even accepted, and be joined to the "day world" of their community. Fashion, once understood only as the commodity playground of the wealthy, might be understood as the art form it actually is. That is already happening: Alexander McQueen's tragic death spawned museum and gallery showings of his work, once referred to as "outlandish," now better understood as the work of a genius. Fashion and fetish also must be understood as one: fashion is the fetish of people for whom the beauty and craft they long to see coalesces in the world of fashion. And fetishists already understand that their fetish is a matter of fashion, first and foremost. But I think everyone involved in this adoration of fashion, costume, performance, and fetish hopes that this potential moment of acceptance does not in any way spoil the delicious difference that it occupies from the mundane world of the "vanilla" community—that its mystery, humor, eroticism, and exotic allure be allowed to continue as the special province of the devotee.

Notes

Chapter 1: Introduction

1. William Pietz. "Introduction." *Fetishism as Cultural Discourse*. Ed. By Emily Apter and William Pietz (Ithaca and London: Cornell University Press: 1993).
2. Amanda Fernbach, *Fantasies of Fetishism: From Decadence to the Post-Human* (New Brunswick, NJ: Rutgers University Press, 2002), 183.
3. *Encyclopedia Britannica: Dictionary of Arts, Sciences and General Literature*, 9th ed. B, vol. 9: FAL–FYZ (New York: The Henry G. Allen Co., 1890), 118–19, s.v. "Fetichism."
4. Ibid.
5. Paraphrased in William Pietz, in "Fetishism and Materialism," Apter and Pietz, in Fetishism as Cultural Discourse (Ithaca, NY: Cornell University Press, 1993), 138. (1985): 7.
6. *Encyclopedia Britannica*, 119.
7. Emily Apter, "Introduction," in *Fetishism as Cultural Discourse*, ed. Emily Apter and William Pietz (Ithaca, NY: Cornell University Press, 1993), 6.
8. *Encyclopedia Britannica*, 118.
9. Charles Bernheimer, "Fetishism and Decadence: Salome's Severed Heads," in Apter and Pietz, *Fetishism as Cultural Discourse*, 63.
10. Pietz, "Problem of Fetish," 11.
11. *Encyclopedia Britannica*, 118.
12. Carlton J.H. Hayes, Marshall Whithed Baldwin, and Charles Woolsey Cole, *History of Western Civilization*, 2nd ed. (New York and London: The Macmillan Company, 1967), 621.
13. James Laver, *The Concise History of Costume and Fashion* (New York: Harry N. Abrams, Inc., 2002), 211.
14. Anne McClintock, *Imperial Leather: Race, Gender and Sexuality in the Colonial Conquest* (New York and London: Routledge, 1995), 174.
15. Mistress Jean Bardot, interview with author, October 21, 2010.
16. Ground Zero (a nightclub at 15 Fourth Street Northeast, Minneapolis, Minnesota) has a fetish performance on Saturday nights at midnight. In the past, it was directed by Mistress Jean Bardot and her group of dominatrices. In 2010, she gave up directing to another to work on her international performance schedule.

17. Those who like to be walked or stood on. The two such subjects I interviewed were heterosexual men and like to have women "trample" them. This particular fetish is not currently listed in the *Diagnostic and Statistical Manual of Mental Disorders: DSM-IV.*
18. "Vanilla" is the moniker given to all non-fetishists who are ignorant of the fetish performance and fetishists.
19. Ulrich Lehmann, *Tigersprung: Fashions in Modernity* (Cambridge, MA: MIT Press, 2000), 285.
20. Cristina Degli-Esposti, "Sally Potter's *Orlando* and the Neo-Baroque Scopic Regime," *Cinema Journal* 36, no. 1 (Autumn 1996): 80, http://www.jstor.org/stable/1225596 (accessed September 2010).

Chapter 2: Fetish Style History

1. Ulrich Lehmann. *Tigersprung: Fashion in Modernity*. (Cambridge, Massachusetts: The MIT Press, 2000), 91.
2. Robert Nye, "Medical Origins of Sexual Fetishism," in *Fetishism as Cultural Discourse*, ed. Emily Apter and William Pietz (Ithaca, NY: Cornell University Press, 1993), 13–30.
3. Ibid., 15.
4. Ibid.
5. Ibid.
6. Ibid., 17.
7. Ibid., 18.
8. Ibid., 21.
9. Quoted in Ibid., 22.
10. Ibid., 28.
11. Ibid.
12. Ibid., 30.
13. This description was quoted in Nye, "Medical Origins of Sexual Fetishism," and sounds much like a description of the contemporary Superman superhero of the American comic book, but in fact, it was taken from Joris-Karl Huysmans's *A rebours* (Paris: Fasquelle, n.d.), 140.
14. *Encyclopedia Americana*, vol. 29 (Danbury, CT: Grolier, 1993), 106, s.v. "Woman Suffrage."
15. Patrick Kay Bidelman, *Pariahs Stand Up! The Founding of the Liberal Feminist Movement in France, 1858–1889* (Westport, CT, and London: Greenwood Press, 1982), 3.
16. Ibid., 4.
17. Hubertine Auclert, *Historique de la société le droit des femmes 1876–1880* (Paris, 1881), 19.

18. Bidelman, *Pariahs Stand Up!*, 4–5. In this section, Bidelman also recounts a story that somewhere in a museum is a chair that Napoleon ripped and gashed while in a rage when confronted with the criticism that he had been too harsh on women.

19. Ibid., 14–15.

20. Anne McClintock, *Imperial Leather: Race, Gender and Sexuality in the Colonial Conquest* (New York and London: Routledge, 1995), 98.

21. Bidelman, *Pariahs Stand Up!*, 18.

22. McClintock, *Imperial Leather*, 174.

23. Quoted in Rosalind H. Williams, *Dream Worlds: Mass Consumption in Late Nineteenth-Century France* (Berkeley: University of California Press, 1982), 5.

24. Ibid., 3.

25. Jonathan Crary, *Techniques of the Observer: On Vision and Modernity in the Nineteenth Century* (Cambridge, MA: MIT Press, 1995), 127.

26. Williams, *Dream Worlds*, 11.

27. McClintock, *Imperial Leather*, 210.

28. Ibid., 208.

29. Philip B. Meggs and Alston W. Purvis, *Meggs' History of Graphic Design*, 5th ed. (Hoboken, NJ: John Wiley & Sons, 2012), 201.

30. Ibid.

31. Ibid., 202.

32. Ibid.

33. Neil McKendrick, John Brewer, and J.H. Plumb, *The Birth of a Consumer Society: The Commercialization of Eighteenth Century England* (Bloomington: University of Indiana Press, 1982), 41.

34. Ibid., 45.

35. Ibid., 46.

36. Ibid.

37. McClintock, *Imperial Leather*, 212.

38. Ibid., 213.

39. McKendrick, Brewer, and Plumb, *Consumer Society*, 52.

40. Ibid., 55.

41. Ibid., xx.

42. Ibid., 9.

43. Quoted in Valerie Steele. *Paris Fashion: A Cultural History* (Oxford: Berg Publishers, 1998), 24.

44. Ibid.

45. Daniel Purdy, "Introduction," in *The Rise of Fashion: A Reader*, ed. Daniel Purdy (Minneapolis: University of Minnesota Press, 2004), 7.

46. Norbert Elias, "Etiquette and Ceremony: Conduct and Sentiment of Human Beings as functions of the Power Structure of Their Society" from *The Court Society* (1969) in Purdy, *The Rise of Fashion*, 52.

47. Ibid.
48. Valerie Steele, *Paris Fashion: A Cultural History* (New York and Oxford: Oxford University Press, 1988), 32–33.
49. Lehmann, *Tigersprung*, 311.
50. Ibid.
51. Quoted in Sarah S.G. Frantz, "The First Truly Modern Celebrity," review of *Beau Brummell: The Ultimate Man of Style*, in "Book Reviews," ed. Sue Parrill, *JASNA News* 22, no. 3 (Winter 2006): 27, http://www.jasna.org/bookrev/br223p27.html (accessed December 19, 2010).
52. "Early redingotes appeared in the late 1780s and were versatile enveloping full-length overcoats. The English redingote was made of good woolen cloth and was generally lightweight, but it also had shoulder capes and buttoned across the chest. It was popular in many forms through the 19th century and basically began life as an outdoor riding coat for inclement weather . . . Redingotes were used alongside mantles and cloaks for everyday wear often because they were practical, utilitarian, unfussy and unnoticeable compared to more ostentatious lavishly trimmed clothes. They were of course also used for riding." Pauline Weston Thomas, "Redingote and Riding Coat Pictures 1 Fashion History," http://www.fashion-era.com/Coats_history/redingote_history_1.htm (accessed July 18, 2010).
53. Lehmann, *Tigersprung*, 313.
54. François Boucher, *20,000 Years of Fashion: The History of Costume and Personal Adornment* (New York: Harry N. Abrams, 1966), 363.
55. J.C. Flügel, "The Great Masculine Renunciation and Its Causes," in Purdy, *The Rise of Fashion*, 103.
56. Charles Baudelaire, "The Painter of Modern Life," in *The Painter of Modern Life and Other Essays*, 2nd ed., trans. and ed. Jonathan Mayne (London: Phaidon Press, 1995), 27–28.
57. Lehmann, *Tigersprung*, 321.
58. Baudelaire, "Painter," 26.
59. Ibid., 28.
60. Lehmann, *Tigersprung*, 6.
61. Charles Baudelaire, "Salon de 1846, XVIII," *Oeuvres completes*, 494; trans. J. Mayne in Baudelaire, *Art in Paris, 1845–1862: Salons and Other Exhibitions Reviewed by Charles Baudelaire* (Oxford: Phaidon, 1965), 117. Translation modified by Lehmann, *Tigersprung*, 27.
62. Lehmann, *Tigersprung*, 39.
63. Flügel, "Great Masculine Renunciation," 104.
64. Ibid.
65. Ibid., 105.
66. Lehmann, *Tigersprung*, 39.
67. Boucher, *20,000 Years of Fashion*, 388.

68. Ibid.
69. Ibid., 366.
70. Steele, *Paris Fashion*, 147.
71. Boucher, *20,000 Years of Fashion*, 388.
72. Daniel Leonhard Purdy, "Feminist Dress Reform," in Purdy, *Rise of Fashion*, 109.
73. Ibid.
74. Steele, *Paris Fashion*, 195.
75. Boucher, *20,000 Years of Fashion*, 394.
76. Ibid.
77. Lehmann, *Tigersprung*, 9.
78. Valerie Steele, *Fetish: Fashion, Sex & Power* (New York: Oxford University Press, 1996), 51.
79. Boucher, *20,000 Years of Fashion*, 355.
80. Ibid., 376.
81. McClintock, *Imperial Leather*, 33.
82. Ibid., 160.
83. Michel Foucault, *The History of Sexuality*, vol. 1, *An Introduction* (New York: Vintage Books, 1990), 47.
84. Frenchy Lunning, "Under the Ruffles: Shôjo and the Morphology of Power," in *Mechademia 6: User Enhanced*, ed. Frenchy Lunning (Minneapolis: University of Minnesota Press, 2011), 13. The four paragraphs consisting of this quotation and the previous paragraphs were part of a discussion of the Japanese "Lolita" character but are also appropriate for this discussion.
85. Paraphrased from Valerie Steele, *Fashion and Eroticism: Ideals of Feminine Beauty from the Victorian Era to the Jazz Age* (New York: Oxford University Press, 1985), chapter 9, 57.
86. "An Overview of Underwear," in *The Ladies Treasury of Costume and Fashion*. © Copyright 2002–2005 The Ladies Treasury, http://www.tudorlinks.com/treasury/articles/viewvictunder1.html (accessed September 7, 2010).
87. Ibid.
88. David Kunzle, *Fashion and Fetishism: Corsets, Tightlacing & Other Forms of Body Sculpture* (Gloucestershire: Sutton Publishing, 2006), 81.
89. Ibid., 164–65.
90. "Overview of Underwear."
91. Ibid.
92. Ibid.
93. Ibid.
94. Quoted in Steele, *Fashion and Eroticism*, 88.
95. Ibid., 89.
96. Ibid., 93.
97. Ibid., 87.

98. Ibid.

99. The dates used here came from: Robert V. Beinvenu II, "The Development of Sadomasochism as a Cultural Style in the Twentieth-Century United States" (PhD diss., University of Indiana, 1998), 15–17.

100. Ibid., 42.

101. Ibid., 17.

102. Ibid.

103. Ibid.

104. Rebecca Arnold, *Fashion, Desire and Anxiety: Image and Morality in the 20th Century* (New Brunswick, NJ: Rutgers University Press, 2001), 56.

105. In e-mail conversations with Dr. Timothy Perper, I received some additional reminders of key events of that radical and eventful period.

106. "Stonewall Rebellion," *The New York Times*, Tuesday, May 17, 2011, Times Topics, http://topics.nytimes.com/topics/reference/timestopics/subjects/s/stonewall_rebellion/index.html (accessed September 2010).

107. Sandra Niessen, "Compte rendu: GAINES, Jane, HERZOG, Charlotte (eds). Fabrications: Costume and the Female Body. New York: Routledge, 1990, 295p," *Cinémas: revue d'études cinématographiques/Cinémas: Journal of Film Studies* 3, nos. 2–3 (1993): 247–51; www.erudit.org/revue/cine/1993/v3/n2-3/1001202ar.pdf (accessed October 2010).

108. "Critical Theory" in *Key Concepts in Cultural Theory*, ed. Andrew Edgar and Peter Sedgwick (London and New York: Routledge, 1999), 295.

109. "Paris May–June 1968," *France History Archive*, http://www.marxists.org/history/france/may-1968/ (accessed September–October, 2010.

110. "Critical Theory" 91–92.

111. Ibid., 158.

112. Amanda Fernbach, *Fantasies of Fetishism: From Decadence to the Post-Human* (New Brunswick, NJ: Rutgers University Press, 2002), 20.

113. Vince Brewton, "Literary Theory," in *Internet Encyclopedia of Philosophy: A Peer-Reviewed Academic Resource*, June 29, 2005, http://www.iep.utm.edu/literary/. (Accessed October 2010).

114. Susan K. Donovan, "Luce Irigaray," in *Internet Encyclopedia of Philosophy: A Peer-Reviewed Academic Resource*, July 2, 2005, http://www.iep.utm.edu/irigaray/. (Accessed October 2010).

115. Judith Butler, interview by Peter Osborne and Lynne Segal, "Extracts from *Gender as Performance: An Interview with Judith Butler*" (London: theory.org.uk, 1993; Radical Philosophy, Ltd., 1994), http://www.theory.org.uk/but-int1.htm. (Accessed October 2010).

116. Jason Boog, "Madonna Tops 100 Most Sought After Out-of-Print Books List," in *Galleycat: The First Word of the Book Publishing Industry*; http://www.mediabistro.com/galleycat/madonna-tops-100-most-sought-after-out-of-print-books-list_b13072 (accessed October 2010).

117. Arnold, *Fashion, Desire and Anxiety*, 3.

118. The term *bro* had been the African American form of address for one male to another male, as slang for "brother." It was since assimilated into white culture in the late 1990s and early twenty-first century to refer to a certain type of American young male: white, usually blondish hair, arrogant, upper-middle class, and always dressed in the casual attire of cargo shorts, polo shirt, and either sandals or tennis shoes. He represents the "hound" in bars looking for female attention and the epitome of "cool" for a certain aspect of middle-class culture. It is this image of the "bro-ski" that most older middle-age men emulate, though obviously missing the mark. And despite looking rather pathetic, virtually all men of this age, when dressed casually, will wear some version of this uniform.

119. Fernbach, *Fantasies of Fetishism*, 31.

120. Arnold, *Fashion, Desire and Anxiety*, 72.

121. "Scotland Road Group Proudly Presents The Mods and Rockers," April 11, 2002. Scotland Road Group, http://www.stthomasu.ca/~pmccorm/modsandrockers1.html (accessed November 24, 2011).

122. Ibid.

123. Ibid.

124. Ibid.

125. Ibid.

126. Arnold, *Fashion, Desire and Anxiety*, 74.

127. Ibid.

128. Ibid., 47.

129. Ibid., 13.

130. Ibid.

131. Ibid., 24.

132. Ibid., 47.

133. Ibid., 116.

134. "The New Romantics," *Squidoo*, 2011, http://www.squidoo.com/new-romantics.

135. Arnold, *Fashion, Desire and Anxiety*, 116.

136. The Oxford Dictionary Online states, "The combining form uni- does normally mean 'one, having or consisting of one': it comes from Latin unus 'one.' It forms words such as unicycle, a term for a cycle with just one wheel, and unicellular, meaning 'consisting of a single cell.' And in fact the 20-volume historical Oxford English Dictionary contains entries for the words unisexual, meaning 'of one sex or relating to one sex' and unisexuality, meaning 'the state of being unisexual.' Both these words date back to the early 19th century. Unisex is a much newer word: it was coined in the 1960s and originally used in relatively informal contexts. Its formation seems to have been influenced by words such as union, united, and universal, from which it took the sense of something that was shared. So unisex can be

understood as referring to one thing (such as a clothing style or hairstyle) that is shared by both sexes." Oxford Dictionaries, Oxford University Press, 2011, December 4, 2011, s.v. "Uni-sex," http://oxforddictionaries.com/page/ unisexmeaning?view=uk (accessed February 2011).

137. Arnold, *Fashion, Desire and Anxiety*, 121.
138. Ibid., 117.
139. Caroline Evans, *Fashion at the Edge: Spectacle, Modernity and Deathliness* (New Haven, CT: Yale University Press, 2003), 20.
140. Ibid.
141. Ibid., 24.
142. Ibid., 29.
143. Ibid., 54.

Chapter 3: Fetish Identity

1. Ulrich Lehmann, *Tigersprung: Fashion in Modernity* (Cambridge, MA: MIT Press, 2000), 169.
2. Ibid., 18–19.
3. Valerie Steele, *Paris Fashion: A Cultural History* (New York and Oxford: Oxford University Press, 1988), 164.
4. Anne McClintock, *Imperial Leather: Race, Gender and Sexuality in the Colonial Conquest* (New York and London: Routledge, 1995), 174.
5. Karl Kraus, "The Eroticism of Clothes," in Daniel Purdy, *The Rise of Fashion: A Reader* (Minneapolis: University of Minnesota Press, 2004), 242.
6. Ibid.
7. Ibid., 243.
8. Ibid.
9. Ibid., 244.
10. Daniel Purdy, ed., *The Rise of Fashion: A Reader* (Minneapolis: University of Minnesota Press, 2004), 194.
11. Steele, *Paris Fashion*, 43.
12. Ibid., 44.
13. Quoted in Ibid, 46.
14. Ibid.
15. Lehmann, *Tigersprung*, 25.
16. "George Bryan Brummel (England, 1778–1840)," *Historical Boys Clothing*, May 20, 2002, http://histclo.com/bio/b/bio-brum.html (accessed February 24, 2011).
17. Lehmann, *Tigersprung*, 311.
18. Ibid.
19. Quoted in Ibid., 156.

20. Quoted in Lehmann, *Tigersprung,* 442n71.
21. Ibid., 158.
22. Ibid., 158.
23. Ibid., 160.
24. Ibid., 159.
25. Over the past two years (2009–2011), I have interviewed many fetishists and read discussions of the origin of their fetish obsessions in forums online. An overwhelming majority reveal a seminal vision or narrative that occurred in childhood, in which an object involved in that scene became the "talisman" or "totem" of that experience, forever linked seamlessly with the erotic experience.
26. McClintock, *Imperial Leather,* 202–3.
27. Ibid., 138.
28. Amanda Fernbach, *Fantasies of Fetishism: From Decadence to the Postmodern* (New Brunswick, NJ: Rutgers University Press, 2002), 227–28.
29. McClintock, *Imperial Leather,* 224.
30. Ibid., 160.
31. Ibid., 161.
32. *"La scène est dans un boudoir délicieux!"* Donatien Alphonse François, Marquis de Sade, "Troiseme dialogue [Madame de Saint-Ange, Eugénie, Dolmancé]," in *Oeuvres completes,* ed. Gilbert Lely, 16 vols. (Paris, 1966–1967), 3: 381.
33. McClintock, *Imperial Leather,* 184.
34. *The American Heritage Dictionary of the English Language,* 4th ed. (Houghton Mifflin Company, 2004); Answers.com, http://www.answers.com/topic/boudoir (accessed February 27, 2011), s.v. "boudoir."
35. Emily Apter, "Cabinet Secrets: Fetishism, Prostitution, and the Fin de Siècle Interior," Assemblage 9 (June 1989): 6–19, http://www.jstor.org/stable/3171149.
36. Kathleen Kete, *The Beast in the Boudoir: Petkeeping in Nineteenth-century Paris* (Berkeley: University of California Press, 1994), 2–3.
37. Apter, "Cabinet Secrets," 8.
38. Ibid., 9.
39. Ibid., 10.
40. Ed Lilley, "The Name of the Boudoir," *Journal of the Society of Architectural Historians* 53, no. 2 (June 1994): 196.
41. Ibid., 193.
42. Apter, "Cabinet Secrets," 14.
43. Ibid., 14–15.
44. Ibid., 15. Apter cites this salacious little quote from Gustave Droz. In French: *"Que votre nid soit douillet, qu'on vous sente dans tous ces mille riens."*
45. Ibid.
46. Ibid.
47. Ibid., 16.

48. Anne McClintock, "Maid to Order: Commercial Fetishism and Gender Power," *Social Text, No. 37: A Special Section Edited by Anne McClintock Explores the Sex Trade* (Winter 1993): 87.

49. McClintock, *Imperial Leather*, 143.

50. Ibid., 142.

51. Ibid., 144.

52. Fernbach, *Fantasies of Fetishism*, 183.

53. Ibid., 191.

54. McClintock, *Imperial Leather*, 319.

55. Fernbach, *Fantasies of Fetishism*, 193.

56. McClintock, "Maid to Order," 91.

57. McClintock, *Imperial Leather*, 319.

58. McClintock, "Maid to Order," 95.

59. Ibid., 107.

60. Ibid., 100.

61. Ibid., 106.

62. Timothy Scheie, "Body Trouble: Corporeal Presence and Performative Identity in Cixou's and Mnouchkine's 'L'Indiade ou l'Inde de leurs rêves,'" *Theatre Journal* 46, no. 1 (1994): 33.

63. Judith Butler, "Bodies That Matter," in *Feminist Theory and the Body: A Reader*, ed. Janet Price and Margrit Shildrick (New York and London: Routledge, 1999), 235–37.

64. Fernbach, *Fantasies of Fetishism*, 193.

65. Laura Mulvey, "Some Thoughts on Theories of Fetishism in the Context of Contemporary Culture," *October 65* (Summer 1993): 3–20, http://www.jstor.org/stable/778760 (accessed December 2011).

66. Ibid., 8.

67. Ibid., 5–6.

68. Robert Stam, Robert Burgoyne, and Sandy Flitterman-Lewis, *New Vocabularies in Film Semiotics: Structuralism, Post-structuralism and Beyond* (London and New York: Routledge, 1992), 137.

69. Ibid., 148.

70. Mulvey, "Some Thoughts," 6.

71. Ibid., 7.

72. Ibid.

73. Caroline Evans, *Fashion at the Edge: Spectacle, Modernity and Deathliness* (New Haven, CT: Yale University Press, 2003), 51, 53.

74. Mulvey, "Some Thoughts," 13.

75. Ibid., 12.

76. Emily Apter, *Feminizing the Fetish: Psychoanalysis and Narrative Obsession in Turn-of-the-Century France* (Ithaca, NY, and London: Cornell University Press, 1991), 70.

77. Joan Copjec, "The Sartorial Superego," *October 50* (Fall 1988): 57–96, quoted in Apter, *Feminizing the Fetish*, 81.

78. Mary Ann Doane, *The Desire to Desire: The Woman's Film of the 1940s* (London: Macmillan Press, 1987), 30, 32.

79. Apter, *Feminizing the Fetish*, 81.

80. Mulvey, "Some Thoughts," 19.

81. Ibid., 20.

Chapter 4: Fetish Style: Fetish as Fashion

1. Eugénie Lemoine-Luccioni, *La Robe* (Paris: Seuil, 1983), 34. Quoted in Marjorie Garber, "Fetish Envy," *October 54* (Autumn 1990): 45–56, http://www.jstor.org/stable/778668 (accessed May 2011).

2. Angelika Rauch, "The *Trauerspiel* of the Prostituted Body, or Woman as Allegory of Modernity," *Cultural Critique* 10, *Popular Narrative, Popular Images* (Autumn 1988): 85–86, http://www.jstor.org/stable/1354107 (accessed May 27, 2011).

3. Merriam-Webster, http://www.merriam-webster.com/dictionary/clothing (accessed May 26, 2011), s.v. "clothing" (accessed April 2011).

4. *Columbia Encyclopedia*, the Columbia Electronic Encyclopedia, 6th ed. (Columbia University Press, 2011), www.cc.columbia.edu/cu/cup/. Quoted by Answers.com, http://www.answers.com/topic/costume (accessed May 16, 2011), s.v. "costume."

5. Piers D. G. Britton, "Dress and the Fabric of the Television Series: The Costume Designer as Author in *Dr. Who*," *Journal of Design History* 12, no. 4 (1999): 347, http://www.jstor.org/stable/1316242 (accessed May 2011).

6. Félix Guattari arrived at this term to be used by "groups creatively autoproducing themselves as they adapt, cross, communicate and travel, in short, as they traverse different levels, segments, and roles," and it will be discussed later in this chapter. Gary Genosko, *Félix Guattari: An Aberrant Introduction* (London and New York: Continuum, 2002), 55.

7. Garber, "Fetish Envy," 46.

8. Lyn Cowan, *Masochism: A Jungian View* (Ann Arbor, MI: Spring Publications, 1982), 54.

9. Marjorie Garber, *Vested Interests: Cross-dressing and Cultural Anxiety* (New York: Routledge, 1997), 12.

10. *Britannica Concise Encyclopedia* (Encyclopædia Britannica, Inc., 1994–2011), http://www.answers.com/topic/fashion#ixzz1Nl3aa0vP (accessed May 26, 2011), s.v. "fashion."

11. "Diagnosis Dictionary: Fetishism," *Psychology Today*, October 24, 2005, http://www.psychologytoday.com/conditions/fetishism (accessed June 1, 2011).

12. Mistress Jean Bardot, interview with author, October 21, 2010.

13. Dr. John Money, quoted in "Paraphilic Infantilism," *Understanding Infantilism. org*, http://understanding.infantilism.org/essay.php (accessed February 2011).

14. *Zentai* suits (from the Japanese ゼンタイ, meaning "whole or entire") is a term for skin-tight garments that cover the entire body or "skinsuits." The word is a contraction of *zenshin taitsu* (全身タイツ, meaning full-body tights"). They are most commonly seen on superhero costumes and athletic uniforms for cross-country skiing and similar sports.

15. Louise J. Kaplan, *Cultures of Fetishism* (New York and Basingstoke: Palgrave Macmillan, 2006), 74.

16. Ibid., 75.

17. Ibid., 74.

18. Valerie Steele, *Fetish: Fashion, Sex & Power* (New York: Oxford University Press, 1996), 57.

19. Michel Foucault, "Text, Discourse, Ideology," in *Untying the Text*, ed. Robert Young (New York and London: Routledge Kegan & Paul, 1982), 48.

20. Cowan, *Masochism*, 75.

21. Kaplan, *Cultures of Fetishism*, 91.

22. Steele, *Fetish*, 58.

23. To explain the nebulous descriptions of the merry widow extant, a rather randy description on an online catalog does it best: "This lacy plus sized corset is perfect for under a wedding gown—or whenever you want sexy support. There is some debate on the difference between a corset and a merry widow, so we say call it whichever name sounds sexier to you. Form-fitting and supportive, this merry widow has lightly lined cups, boning for support and detachable garters. Merry widows aren't just for wedding gowns either. For some old Hollywood glamour wear it with a pair of sexy lace top thigh highs and marabou pumps. Become a naughty After Hours. Nurse with this corset under your nursing uniform with stockings and white patent stilettos. Either way, this versatile piece of plus size lingerie is a must have!" "Lace Merry Widow," http://www.hipsandcurves.com/plus-size-lingerie/ (accessed November 2010).

24. Todd McFarlane, *Spawn I* (New York: Random House Trade, 1998).

25. Steele, *Fetish*, 68.

26. Louis Fleischauer, http://louisfleischauer.com/Human_Instruments.html (accessed 2010; text has since been deleted).

27. "History of Vinyl," *Vinyl Institute*, http://www.vinylinfo.org/vinyl-info/about-vinyl/history-of-vinyl/ (accessed September 2011).

28. "Domina Dress ABBESS," *Marquis Bazaar Bizarre*, http://www.marquis.de/onlineshop/default.php?cPath=21_45_47_56&page=2 (accessed October 2011).

29. "Vacuum & Bodybags," *Marquis Bazaar Bizarre*, http://www.marquis.de/onlineshop/default.php?cPath=32_84 (accessed October 2011).

30. *Marquis Bazaar Bizarre*, http://www.marquis.de/onlineshop/product_info.php?
    cPath=21_45_47_56&products_id=810 (accessed October 2011).
31. *American Heritage Dictionary*, 3rd ed. (New York: Laurel Book, 1994), 414,
    s.v. "identity."
32. Andrew Edgar and Peter Sedgwick, eds., *Key Concepts in Cultural Theory*
    (London and New York: Routledge, 2002), 187.
33. Andrew Edgar and Peter Sedgwick, "Humanism," in Edgar and Sedgwick, *Key
    Concepts in Cultural Theory*, 181.
34. *American Heritage*, 148, s.v. "character."
35. Garber, *Vested Interests*, 29.
36. Ibid., 35.
37. Steele, *Fetish*, 159–60.
38. Garber, *Vested Interests*, 17.
39. Anne McClintock, *Imperial Leather: Race, Gender and Sexuality in the Colo-
    nial Contest* (New York and London: Routledge, 1995), 143.
40. Ulrich Lehmann, *Tigersprung: Fashion in Modernity* (Cambridge, MA: MIT
    Press, 2000), 24.
41. Ibid., 380–81.
42. Wikipedia, "Bowler hat," *Wikimedia Foundation*, http://en.wikipedia.org/wiki/
    Bowler_hat (accessed October 2011).
43. Lehmann, *Tigersprung*, 291.
44. *Diagnostic and Statistical Manual of Mental Disorders: DSM-IV* (Washington,
    DC: American Psychiatric Association, 2000).
45. Thomas John Speaker, "Psychosexual Infantilism in Adults: The Eroticization
    of Regression." PhD diss., Columbia Pacific University, 1986. http://under
    standing.infantilism.org/surveys/ts_doctoral_dissertation_p_6.php (accessed
    February 2011).
46. Tristan Taormino, "Still in Diapers," *The Village Voice Columns*, August 13,
    2002, http://www.villagevoice.com/people/0233,taormino,37378,24.html (ac-
    cessed February 2011).
47. "Small Adult Baby," *Kosmix*, Kosmix Corporation, http://www.kosmix.com/
    topic/small_adult_baby (page no longer available) (accessed February 2011).
48. "Paraphilic Infantilism," in *DSM-IV*, 529.
49. Taormino, "Still in Diapers."
50. The subject "Baby Dani" (pseudonym), interview with author, March 30, 2011,
    Saint Paul, MN.
51. Dr. Thomas O. Sargent, "Fetishism," *Journal of Social Work and Human Sexu-
    ality*, Special Issue, *The Sexually Unusual: Guide to Understanding and Help-
    ing*, 7, no. 1 (1988): 27–42.
52. Interview with "Baby Dani (she changed her name after first interview)."
53. "Paraphilic Infantilism," *Wikipedia* (Wikimedia Foundation 2006), http://
    en.wikipedia.org/wiki/Paraphilic_infantilism. There are also "babyfurs," which

are AB or AB/DLs who are allied with the "furry fandom": those who fetishize the wearing of fur and fur-like synthetics (accessed September 2011).

54. Ground Zero (a nightclub at 15 Fourth Street Northeast, Minneapolis, Minnesota).

55. "Windelbodys," *Privatina.eu*, http://81.169.162.205/privatina-s93h186-onsies. html?sid=abd0609ca91f53cc0f1113ce89dc3adc (accessed May 2012).

56. Amanda Fernbach, *Fantasies of Fetishism: From Decadence to the Post-Human* (New Brunswick, NJ: Rutgers University Press, 2002), 27.

57. Rachel Kane, "WTForever 21: Sexy Baby Shorts," *Huffpost Style*: *Huffington Post*, December 8, 2010, http://www.huffingtonpost.com/rachel-kane/wtforever-21-sexy-baby-sh_b_793895.html (accessed May 2012).

58. *American Heritage Dictionary*, 3rd ed. (New York: Laurel Book, 1994), 270, s.v. "effectuation."

59. Tina Chanter, *The Picture of Abjection: Film, Fetish, and the Nature of Difference* (Bloomington and Indianapolis: Indiana University Press, 2008), 6.

60. Steele, *Fetish*, 133.

61. The Furries: "No standard definition exists but generally furries are people who have a fascination with anthropomorphic animals. These are animals that are given human traits, like walking and talking. They can be anything from cartoons characters like Bugs Bunny to computer game personalities like Pokemon. The scene has its own art, animation, comic books and literature, but activities are largely conducted online—where furries adopt 'fursonas' for role playing. But for some it is about meeting other furries in person. Groups around the world meet regularly and there are conventions in the US, UK, Germany, Mexico, France, Russia and Brazil . . . But, inevitably perhaps, there's a sexual element too . . . Some furries assume animal traits—known as zoomorphism—and indentify *[sic]* strongly with certain species. This can range from adopting an online persona to wearing a tail or full-sized fur suits." Denise Winterman, "Who Are the Furries?" *BBC News Magazine*, November 13, 2009, http://news.bbc.co.uk/2/hi/8355287.stm (accessed April 2012).

62. Steele, *Fetish*, 96.

63. Ibid., 98.

64. Ibid., 101.

65. Ibid., 106.

66. Ibid., 109.

67. Henry Krips, *Fetish: An Erotics of Culture* (Ithaca, NY: Cornell University Press, 1999), 10.

68. Ibid.

69. Ibid., 17.

70. *Marquis Bazaar Bizarre* http://www.marquis.de/onlineshop/default.php?cPath=21 (accessed April 2012).

Chapter 5: Fetish Style: Fashion as Fetish

1. Georg Simmel, "Fashion" in *The Rise of Fashion: A Reader*, edited by Daniel Leonhard Purdy (Minneapolis and London: The University of Minnesota Press, 2004), 295.

2. Amanda Fernbach, *Fantasies of Fetishism: From Decadence to the Post-human* (New Brunswick, NJ: Rutgers University Press, 2002), 4.

3. The website states the dress code succinctly: "The best and yet most simple argument supporting the idea of a dresscode is, that the eye prefers a flamboyant, styled and colourful crowd in favour against the ordinary 'jeans and tshirt' look. So, in general, dresscode means: NOT your average everyday life clothing! You can check out if there is a dresscode to an event by having a look at the 'Dates' section, lots of tips and tricks, whats favourable and possible can be found here!" "Dresscode," *KitKatClub Berlin*, http://www.kitkatclub.org/Home/Club/Index.en.html (accessed March 2012).

4. Quoted in Ulrich Lehmann, *Tigersprung: Fashions in Modernity* (Cambridge, MA: MIT Press, 2000), 150.

5. Ibid., 169.

6. Fernbach, *Fantasies of Fetishism*, 10.

7. Ibid., 13.

8. Lehmann, *Tigersprung*, 170.

9. Caroline Evans, *Fashion at the Edge: Spectacle, Modernity and Deathliness* (New Haven, CT: Yale University Press, 2003), 89–90.

10. Simon Reynolds, "The Songs of Now Sound a Lot Like Then," *New York Times*, July 17, 2011.

11. Ibid.

12. A comment by Ursula Murray-Husted made me ponder this phrase, which seems to work for many things beyond television. The "original meaning was the point when a television series shows it has run out of ideas and must resort to stunts to retain viewer interest. Derived from a scene in the last years of Happy Days when the Fonz waterskied over a shark. Includes actions such as 'it was all a dream' episodes, live episodes, lead actors playing guest characters, and putting entire cast into a parody of some pop cultural event." *Urban Dictionary*, "Jump the Shark," http://www.urbandictionary.com/define.php?term=jump+the+shark (accessed March 2012).

13. Kate Alexandra MacLeish, "Fashion News: Malcolm McClaren RIP," Manchester Fashion Network, Quotes from Brainyquote.com, http://www.manchesterfashion.com/c/19/348/malcolm-macclaren-rip/ (accessed 1/10/2013).

14. A merry widow is a foundation garment that covers the breasts and extends down to cover the genitals, and although it forms the shape of the corset, it is not for tight-lacing but simply for highly feminine erotic emphasis. Usually

surrounded in lace and ruffles, it has become popular with manufacturers such as Victoria's Secret for seduction nightwear. It curiously has also been used frequently as a base for the comic book superhero costume—sometimes for the villain as well.

15. Valerie Steele, *Fetish: Fashion, Sex & Power* (New York: Oxford University Press, 1996), 86.
16. Robert Bell, "Vivienne Westwood: 34 Years in Fashion: 12 November 2004–30 January 2005," *National Gallery of Australia.* This essay was first published in *The World of Antiques and Art*, August 2004–February 2005, pp. 14–16, http://nga.gov.au/westwood/article.cfm (accessed April 2012).
17. Claire Wilcox quoted in Robert Bell, "Vivienne Westwood: 34 Years in Fashion: 12 November 2004–30 January 2005," *National Gallery of Australia*, http://nga.gov.au/westwood/Wilessay.cfm (accessed April 2012).
18. Ibid.
19. Chris Brown, "Backstage at Jean Paul Gaultier Menswear," February 3, 2010, *New York Fashion: Latest Shows*, http://nymag.com/fashion/fashionshows/designers/bios/jeanpaulgaultier/ (accessed May 2012).
20. In the eighteenth century, a "panier was initially a stiff underskirt fitted with more or less circular (or dome- or cupola-shaped) boned hoops, worn under the robe volante. It was then divided and took the form of oblong paniers, spreading the fullness of court gowns on either side of the hips." François Boucher, *20,000 Years of Fashion: The History of Costume and Personal Adornment* (New York: Harry N. Abrams, 1966), 295.
21. Evans, *Fashion at the Edge*, 237.
22. Lehmann, *Tigersprung*, 354.
23. Louis W. Marvick, "Fontenelle and the Truth of Masks," *Modern Language Studies* 23, no. 4 (Autumn 1993), 76. http://www.jstor.org/stable/3195206.
24. Quoted in Valerie Steele, Patricia Mears, Yuniya Kawamura, and Hiroshi Narumi, *Japan Fashion Now* (New Haven, CT: Yale University Press, in association with the Fashion Institute of Technology, New York, 2010), 74.
25. Suzy Menkes, "Undercover: Strange, 'but beautiful'—Style—International Herald Tribune," *New York Times—Style*, Wednesday, May 31, 2006, http://www.nytimes.com/2006/04/10/style/10iht-fundercover.1511711.html (accessed March 2012).
26. Huda, "Islamic Clothing Glossary," *About.com—Islam*, http://islam.about.com/od/dress/tp/clothing-glossary.htm (accessed March 2012).
27. See the work on the Algerian war, colonialism, and the veil in the various books by Franz Fanon, in which he posits that Algerian women, who had until the war against colonialism been dressed in modern Western styles, wherein the French military made it a central goal to "uncover" women's perceived role in the revolution, took up the veil as an act of revolution against the French.

28. "Undercover," *Voguepedia: The World of Fashion in Vogue*, Vogue.com, http://www.vogue.com/voguepedia/Undercover (accessed April 2012).

29. An ironic personal note: years ago, a friend and I were walking across a bridge in Boston, Massachusetts, when an extremely attractive man passed us hurriedly in a beautiful Burberry trench coat and attaché case. As he quickly passed us, we remarked at how attractive he was, and suddenly, the wind came up and blew apart the back opening of his beautiful Burberry trench coat to reveal a very nice hairy ass and trouser clips. We laughed so loudly and so long, *we* became the exhibition.

30. Frenchy Lunning, "Cosplay, Drag, and the Performance of Abjection," in *Mangatopia: Essays on Manga and Anime in the Modern World*, ed. Timothy Perper and Martha Cornog (Santa Barbara, CA: ABC-CLIO, Libraries Unlimited, 2011), 71.

31. Fred Patten wrote of his first sighting of cosplayers, stating, "This is also the first (?) convention to include several anime character costumes in its Masquerade, with a group of six San Diego fans led by Karen Schaubelt as *Captain Harlock* and *Star Blazer* characters." This is perhaps inaccurate, as Patten notes by including a question mark after his statement, alluding to his lack of knowledge of this act as the seminal act. But there really is no official documentation of most of these early events. Patten was an early fan and key to many seminal events and conventions where much of the innovations of these fan-based practices occurred. Patten is as close as we get to a primary source for the history of early anime/manga fandom. Lunning, "Cosplay, Drag," 71.

32. *Anime* refers to Japanese animations, whereas *manga* refers to Japanese comic books. Both use a very specific style in drawings and in the visual codes found therein.

33. Lunning, "Cosplay, Drag," 76.

34. Steele, *Fetish*, 64–65.

35. Ibid., 34.

36. Frenchy Lunning, "Under the Ruffles: Shôjo and the Morphology of Power," in *Mechademia 6: User Enhanced*, ed. Frenchy Lunning (Minneapolis: University of Minnesota Press, 2011), 10.

37. Samantha Rei, "Biography," *Blasphemina's Closet*, http://www.blaspheminas closet.com/biography/ (accessed April 2012).

38. Megan Bishop can be found at apatico.net, Heather Luca's work can be found at scoundrelleskeep.com, and Samantha Rei's work at blaspheminascloset.com.

39. Samantha Rei, "blasphemina's photostream," *flickr*, http://www.flickr.com/people/blasphemina/ (accessed April 2012).

40. Shien Lee, *Dances of Vice*, http://dancesofvice.com/ (accessed April 2012).

41. Hajime Sorayama, interview with artist, May 20, 2008, Takayuki Tatsumi, interpreter.

42. Ibid.

Chapter 6: The Future of Fetish Style

1. Cristina Degli-Esposti, "Sally Potter's *Orlando* and the Neo-Baroque Scopic Regime," *Cinema Journal* 36, no. 1 (Autumn 1996): 76–77, http://www.jstor.org/stable/1225596 (accessed February 2011).
2. Ibid., 77.
3. Wikipedia, "Mannerism," *Wikimedia Foundation*, November 9, 2012, http://en.wikipedia.org/wiki/Mannerism (accessed March 2012).
4. Ihab Hassan, "On the Problem of the Postmodern," *New Literary History* 20, no. 1, Critical Reconsiderations (Autumn 1988): 21, http://www.jstor.org/stable/469317 (accessed February 2012).
5. Caroline Evans, *Fashion at the Edge: Spectacle, Modernity and Deathliness* (New Haven, CT: Yale University Press, 2003), 24.
6. Frenchy Lunning, "Cosplay, Drag, and the Performance of Abjection," in *Mangatopia: Essays on Manga and Anime in the Modern World*, ed. Timothy Perper and Martha Cornog (Santa Barbara, CA: ABC-CLIO, Libraries Unlimited, 2011), 85.
7. Kerry Mallan and Roderick McGillis, "Between a Frock and a Hard Place: Camp Aesthetics and Children's Culture," *Canadian Review of American Studies/Revue canadienne d'études américaines* 35, no. 1 (2005): 4.
8. Chris Marshall and Bryan Reynolds, "Transversal Acting," *Semiotic Review of Books* 17, no. 1 (2007): 2.
9. Gary Genosko, *Félix Guattari: An Aberrant Introduction* (London and New York: Continuum, 2002), 71.
10. Lunning, "Cosplay, Drag."
11. Genosko, *Félix Guattari*, 75.
12. Lunning, "Cosplay, Drag."85.
13. Ibid., 84–85.
14. Steven Best and Douglas Kellner, *Postmodern Theory: Critical Interrogations* (New York: Guilford, 1991), 62.

Index